BASICS FOR A
Biblical
WORLDVIEW

bju **press**®

Greenville, South Carolina

Note: The fact that a given writer is cited or quoted in this textbook does not mean that BJU Press endorses that writer from the standpoint of morals, philosophy, or scientific hypotheses. The nature of a worldview book is such that we must cite and quote people with whom we disagree. Part of developing a biblical worldview is cultivating the ability to discern between the good and problematic views of all sorts of people, even Christians.

Basics for a Biblical Worldview, Student Activities Answer Key

Course Vision and Design
Brian Collins, PhD
Bryan Smith, PhD

Writer
Daniel Olachea, MDiv

Consultant
L. Michelle Rosier

Academic Oversight
Jeff Heath, EdD
Rachel Santopietro, MEd

Editor
Suzanne Villegas, MA

Cover and Book Designer
Michael Asire

Cover Illustrator
Karen Schipper

Illustrators
Patrick Mahoney
Rommel Ruiz

Page Layout
Lydia Thompson

Digital Content Management
Peggy Hargis

Permissions
Tatiana Bento
Carrie Hanna

Project Coordinator
Christopher Daniels

Photo credits appear on page 145.

Acknowledgments appear within the notes, which begin on page 143.

The text for this book is set in Adobe Minion Pro, Adobe Myriad Pro, Avenir, Futura and Futura Condensed by URW, and Oswald by Vernon Adams.

ISBN 978-1-62856-630-7

15 14 13 12 11 10 9 8 7 6 5 4 3 2 1

WORLDVIEWS OF THE PAST

Worldviews have existed not only in every place but also in every time. People have always wondered about those big questions: Where did I come from? Why am I here? What's wrong with the world? How can things be made right? Where are we all headed in the end? Because every person throughout time has had a worldview, you can observe various worldviews in biblical accounts of ancient history.

Remember that the things people say and do are based on the big story in their head and on their basic beliefs driven by their loves. Since most people don't explain their worldview to others, you can't know their worldview except by what they say and do. As you look at two scenes from biblical history, you will observe what the people say and do and will come to conclusions about their worldviews.

Read the verses and answer the questions.

MEDITERRANEAN SAILORS (790–750 BC)
Jonah 1:1–16

Jonah was on a ship with sailors from other places who had worldviews different from his. Observe their words and actions to find out about their big stories and basic beliefs.

The Joppa coast, where Jonah launched toward Tarshish

1. What did the sailors' reaction to the storm reveal about their big stories? Who did they believe was in control of the world, and what did they think was the status of humans?

   They believed many gods existed and controlled the world. Humans were at the mercy of the gods but could pray in hopes that the god they worshiped would take care of them.

2. What did the captain's response to Jonah's sleeping reveal about his basic belief about prayer?

   He thought everyone could pray to his own god. He thought prayer may bring favor from a god or might cause a god to save them.

3. What did the sailors do and say that demonstrated their basic beliefs about the cause of storms?

   They decided to cast lots to see whose fault the storm was. They believed storms could be caused by a god's wrath on someone.

4. What did their questions to Jonah reveal about their big stories? What did they think could cause things to go wrong in the world?

They believed Jonah's work, his country, or his people could cause things to go wrong. A god could make bad things happen as punishment on humans.

5. What were their basic beliefs about how to respond to the God who had caused the storm?

They believed that something had to be done to the one who was under God's wrath in order to stop the storm.

6. What were their basic beliefs about the value of life?

Even though they believed Jonah to be at fault for the storm, they were reluctant to take his life by throwing him overboard. They believed that taking Jonah's life possibly meant losing their own.

7. What did their response to the calmed storm reveal about their big stories?

Their big stories about many false gods had changed because of the fear of the Lord. They began to worship the Lord as the true God.

Mars Hill, where Paul preached to the philosophers

ATHENIANS (AD 49)
Acts 17:16–34

Paul was in Athens, the famous Greek city, to preach the gospel. Athenians spent almost all their time studying philosophy. Philosophy is basically an attempt to develop worldviews with human reasoning. It tries to answer those big questions that form a worldview. As a result, many Athenians had well-developed worldviews. Observe their words and actions to find out about their big stories and basic beliefs.

8. What common element in the Athenians' big stories troubled Paul as he looked around the city?

Their big stories included many idols (gods), which they reverenced by placing all around the city.

9. What two types of philosophers are mentioned in verse 18?

Epicureans and Stoics

Basics for a Biblical Worldview

10. What did some of the philosophers call Paul, indicating the conflict between their basic beliefs and his?

babbler

11. What did some of the philosophers say about Paul's preaching, showing that they found his big story to be very different from theirs?

They said he was preaching about strange gods. They said his teaching was new.

12. Verse 21 reveals something about the philosophers' big stories. No matter what they may have *said* their purpose on earth was, how did their *actions* show what they really believed they were on earth to do?

They thought the best way to spend all their time was to tell or hear about new things.

13. What was their main love, revealed in verse 21?

new ideas

14. What did Paul first say of them in his message that demonstrated he recognized their worldview based on their actions of idolatry?

He said they were too superstitious, or very religious.

15. What did the altar to the unknown god reveal about their big stories?

Their big stories allowed for gods they had not yet discovered.

16. What did their search for new things reveal about their basic beliefs about gods?

They believed it was important to find out about gods they did not know yet so that they could continue developing their religion.

17. What did Paul quote from their poets to prove the truth of a big story beginning with God's creation of humans in His image and ending with judgment by Jesus?

"in him we live, and move, and have our being" and "we are also his offspring"

18. What does their response to Paul's message indicate about how the idea of a resurrection fit into their big story?

Some could not believe in a resurrection. Some were not sure but were open to the idea. Some believed and changed the big story they believed.

19. How are you able to recognize the worldview of someone else?

    By thinking about their words and actions, I am able to draw conclusions about their

    worldview (big stories, basic beliefs, or loves).

Basics for a Biblical Worldview

BIG STORY ANSWERS

One of the big stories being told today tries to explain how society became broken and how to fix it. The story doesn't include how life started, but it explains the history of society. It interprets the conflicts in history and proposes a solution. The story goes something like this:

Once upon a time there were many religions, which had a lot of influence in society. These religions had different ideas about right and wrong and about relationships between people and God. These differences caused violent conflicts between religions. The conflicts sometimes affected large numbers of people. But since there is no way to prove scientifically that God exists (so this story goes), it is wrong for people in one religion to persecute those in another religion. The only solution to religious conflicts is for religion to not have influence in public. Religious people can meet with those with similar beliefs as long as they keep their beliefs private. They must not bring those beliefs into the community where people with other faiths also live. The world will find peace when religion stops influencing parts of society like politics and education.

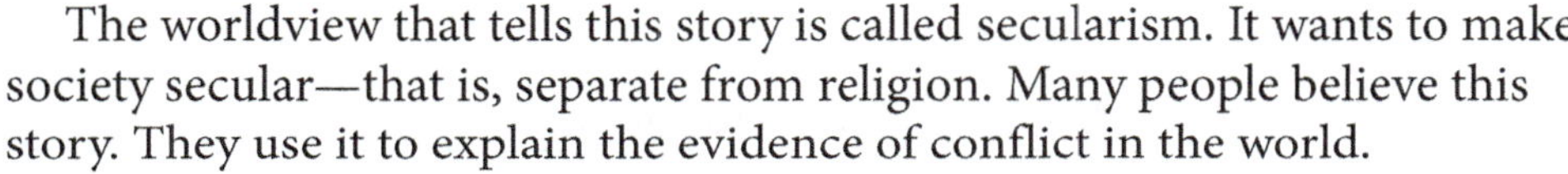

The worldview that tells this story is called secularism. It wants to make society secular—that is, separate from religion. Many people believe this story. They use it to explain the evidence of conflict in the world.

Analyze this big story for its answers to the following big questions of life.

1. Where did society's problems come from?

   differences in religious beliefs

2. Who would be categorized as the "bad guys" in the world?

   religions and the people who persecute people with different religions

3. Who would be categorized as the "good guys"?

   those who keep their religion private and never talk about or use religious ideas in public

4. What is the only way to prove something?

   through science

5. What would be the perfect society?

   The perfect society would have no conflict. Religion, the cause of conflict, would have no influence in the community.

6. How can that perfect society become a reality?

If people are not allowed to bring their religious beliefs into the community, then the community will not have conflicts.

7. What might be considered the purpose of life?

to live in peace with others and to follow whatever religion satisfies you

8. What might be assumed about life after death?

There is probably no life after death because it cannot be proven scientifically.

9. What is the best life that someone could hope for?

to live as long as possible in a society that has eliminated conflict by keeping religion out of community interaction

10. Use some of the questions above to retell a big story that you are familiar with.

Answers should include perceived problems, bad guys, good guys, solutions for problems, and purpose for life.

LOVE AND BELIEFS

You've learned how love affects the way people see things—themselves, other people, stuff, arguments, stories, and God. What you love affects what you truly believe and how you act on those beliefs.

Read the hypothetical scenarios. Evaluate what you are loving in that situation and what your love is making you believe.

1. You steal answers for a test to improve your grades.

   My love for getting good grades or passing the class makes me believe that stealing answers is OK.

2. You give up the TV so that your little sister can watch a show.

   My love for my little sister makes me believe that watching what I want is not as important as sharing with her.

3. You tell someone else about Jesus, even though your friends don't think it's cool.

   My love for Jesus and for the unsaved person makes me believe that my own popularity is not as important as the person's learning about Jesus.

4. You tithe at your church instead of using everything you earned to buy the latest video game.

   My love for God makes me believe that showing gratitude for God's provision is better than having the latest video game.

5. You stay home to finish an assignment for tomorrow while your friends go shopping.

   My love for succeeding in school makes me believe that finishing an assignment on time is more important than seeing new things to buy.

6. You go to church even though you could be at the big game.

   My love for fellowshiping with other believers and worshiping God together makes me believe that it is more important to go to church than to attend the game.

7. You join your friends in smoking even though your parents have told you not to.

My love for my friends' approval or for getting a thrill makes me believe that disobeying my parents is OK.

8. You make friends with a new student who other students think is weird.

My love for my neighbor makes me believe that the new student is more important than the opinions of other students.

9. You choose to spend your time on social media instead of reading your Bible.

My love for entertaining myself or for communicating with friends makes me believe that it is OK to prioritize those things over reading my Bible.

During the career of German scientist Fritz Haber, the world was struggling to produce enough fertilizer to grow the food it needed. The fertilizer that was becoming scarce contained ammonia. Ammonia could be made from the nitrogen in the air, but scientists had not found a way to pull it from the air—until Haber discovered a way. Carl Bosch helped work on the process so that fertilizer could be mass-produced. This process has saved billions of people because of its ability to help grow more crops. It is one of the greatest scientific discoveries of all time. This discovery won Haber the Nobel Prize in Chemistry in 1918.

Not everyone agreed that Haber deserved this award. As a loyal German citizen, Haber had wanted to help his country during World War I. But Germany's actions in the war were against God's law. Haber would have known this through both his Jewish heritage and his Lutheran religion. Yet Haber believed his science was "for humanity in time of peace, for the fatherland [Germany] in time of war." In addition to creating fertilizer, he created explosives and developed a poisonous gas as a weapon. He supervised the first use of his chemical weapon in Belgium to kill Germany's enemies. Haber is now known as the Father of Chemical Warfare.

Haber's life took many tragic turns. His wife committed suicide, possibly because of his work in chemical weapons. His country turned against all Jews, including Haber, during the 1930s. He was exiled from Germany. The rest of Europe condemned his work with chemical weapons. He died in Switzerland with a terrible reputation. His chemicals were eventually used by the Nazis to gas millions of his fellow Jews to death. Haber's own family were some of those killed.

Fritz Haber served the world with science to save billions of lives. His patriotism, however, began to rule his view of right and wrong. He developed terrible weapons that broke international treaties and took the lives of millions.

Answer the questions.

1. How did Fritz Haber help with crop growth?

   He developed a way to get nitrogen out of the air to make ammonia for crop fertilizer.

2. How did Haber help Germany in World War I?

   The process he developed supplied Germany with fertilizer for their crops, he created

   explosives, and he developed poisonous gas as a weapon.

3. How did Haber's work for his country affect his relationship with others?

His work may have been the reason his wife committed suicide, and others were angry with him for developing the chemical weapons.

4. Why did some people dislike that Haber won the Nobel Prize in Chemistry?

because he had used chemistry to develop poisonous gases to kill people

5. In what area was Haber doing good work for humanity?

He did good work solving the problem of how to get enough fertilizer for crops. His work has helped feed billions of people since then.

6. Whom did Haber see as his authority during war?

his country, Germany

7. Based on your evaluation of Haber's beliefs, how would you describe his two-story view?

Haber believed that in war he had to serve his country instead of God. He did not accept that God had authority over everything, including his country, so he made one story for God and one for his country.

8. Based on your evaluation of Haber's actions, how do you think his two-story view came out in each part of his worldview?

He accepted a big story that did not come from the Bible. He loved his country more than God's law, so his beliefs about what he should or should not do changed. As a result, he disobeyed God's law as he worked for his country.

Basics for a Biblical Worldview

You've learned about several things that people use to make sense of their world: a big story, their loves, their authorities, and the way they look at evidence. The following questions will help you draw conclusions from your actions about how *you* make sense of the world. Think carefully and answer honestly based on what you actually think, say, and do—not on what you think should be the "right" answer. See how you make sense of the world.

Answer the questions. *Answers will vary.*

BIG STORY

1. What do you think about when you experience something that you sense is very beautiful?

2. Whom do you blame for things that go wrong in your life?

3. Think of a time when someone did something wrong to you. How did you respond?

4. What gives you hope in your life?

5. Based on your answers to questions 1–4, how would you describe the big story that you are using to make sense of your world?

LOVES

6. When you have time that you can use in any way you want, what do you do?

____

____

7. What kinds of people do you especially like to be around?

____

____

8. When you have money, what do you spend it on?

____

____

9. What job would you like to pursue as an adult?

____

____

10. Based on your answers to questions 6–9, how would you describe your loves that influence how you make sense of your world?

____

____

____

____

AUTHORITY

11. When your friends tell you to do something that you know your parents would not approve, whose advice do you actually follow?

____

____

12. When you are not sure about a decision, whom do you go to first for advice?

____

____

Basics for a Biblical Worldview

13. Think of a time when you changed your mind about something you believed. Who influenced you enough to change your mind?

____

____

14. When you accomplish something, whose approval do you want most for that action?

____

____

15. Based on your answers to questions 11–14, how would you describe the influence of your authorities as you make sense of your world?

____

____

____

____

EVIDENCE

16. You make sense of personal interactions as evidence of how the world truly works. When you see someone do something bad without any consequences, how do you make sense of that?

____

____

17. When you go out of your way to do something right but no one notices, how do you make sense of that?

____

____

18. When someone talks to you with excitement about God, how do you make sense of that?

____

____

19. What personal interactions would you describe as evidence in your sense of friendship?

____

____

20. Based on your answers to questions 16–19, what does your interpretation of evidence show about your sense of the world?

____

____

____

____

Evaluate your answers to the previous questions. *Answers will vary.*

21. What are some areas in which what you *say* you believe about the world is inconsistent with how you really *live* in the world?

____

____

____

____

____

____

____

____

____

OUR BIBLE

Now that you've learned where the Bible came from originally, you might be wondering, *how did we get our Bible in English?*

God used many people to preserve His Word since its initial writing. The Old Testament, written mostly in Hebrew, was preserved by the Jews (Romans 3:1–2). The New Testament, written in Greek, was preserved by local churches as they copied and shared various books with each other. The preservation and spread of the Bible continued through faithful believers who loved the Bible. Over time, the entire Bible has been translated into hundreds of languages, including English. Advancing technology for reading materials helped more and more people access the Bible.

You will follow the process of Scripture preservation in English by researching the following questions. It is a privilege to read God's Word in your own language and to own your own copy. As you research, thank God for His work in many people's lives to accomplish this translation.

Answer the questions with information from your research.

1. In what year was the Wycliffe Bible completed?

   1382

2. What source did John Wycliffe and his followers use for their translation? Why?

   They used the Latin translation called the Vulgate because that was the standard translation in their time, in fact, the only translation allowed by the Roman Catholic Church.

3. What did Johannes Gutenberg develop to print the first book in Europe? Around what year did he invent this?

   movable-type printing press; ca. 1450

4. How were books copied before Gutenberg's development?

   by hand one at a time

5. How did Gutenberg's development improve the spread of the Bible?

   The press made it possible to make many copies much more quickly and cheaply than hand-copied books.

6. During what years did William Tyndale live?

   ca. 1494–1536

7. What sources did Tyndale use for his translation, making it more accurate than Wycliffe's, though he was never able to finish?

   Hebrew and Greek texts

8. In what year was Tyndale's New Testament translation published?

   1525

9. How was Coverdale's Bible connected to the Hebrew and Greek texts? What other sources did it use?

It was partially based on Tyndale's translation from those texts. It also used Luther's German translation and the Latin Vulgate.

10. How was Matthew's Bible connected to the Hebrew and Greek texts? What other sources did it use?

It used Tyndale's translation of portions of the Old Testament and the New Testament from Hebrew and Greek. It used Coverdale's translation of the remaining parts of the Old Testament.

11. In what year was Matthew's Bible first published?

1537

12. In what way was the Geneva Bible's use of the original languages different from previous English translations?

It was the first time that the Old Testament was translated from Hebrew only.

13. In what year was the Geneva Bible first published? In what year was it finally allowed to be printed in England?

1560; 1576

14. What original languages was the King James Bible translated from?

Hebrew and Greek

15. In what year was the King James Bible first published?

1611

The translation of the English Bible was not without cost. Tyndale and some of his associates were burned at the stake. In response to the work and cost involved for you to have your Bible, write a prayer of thanksgiving for this precious gift from God.

Answers will vary but should include an understanding of the work and cost of Bible translation.

English Bible Timeline: Create a timeline using your answers and add two other events from the 1400s to the present that contributed to the history of the English Bible.

Basics for a Biblical Worldview

When you sit down to read a book, you expect the author to follow some sort of plot structure. If there were no characters, no conflict that needed to be sorted out, and no ending, you probably wouldn't even call it a story. The reason you love a good story—and are able to write your own—is that you're made in the image of the Master Storymaker, God Himself.

God planned the story of the world and revealed much of His planning to us in the Bible. If you look carefully at the Bible, you can see the big picture of God's plan. You will see that He *has* and *will* keep all His promises during the unfolding of the story.

Read the verses and answer the questions.

SETTING THE STAGE
Genesis 1:1

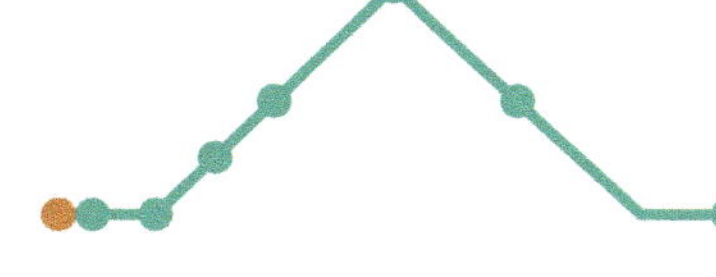

1. What setting did God plan and make for the story of the world?

    the heavens and the earth

> **SUMMARY** God would fill this setting with plants and animals. It is the beginning of all that we know.

CHARACTERS
Genesis 1:26–28

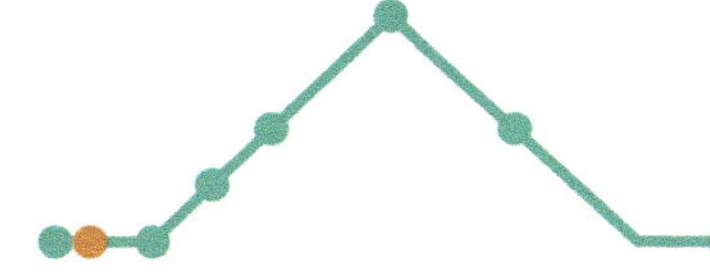

2. Who are the characters God planned in His story?

    humans [Note: Students may also answer "Adam and Eve." Explain that their children would fill the earth to populate God's story.]

3. What was different about the creation of the characters that indicates they would have a greater role in God's plan than the rest of creation?

    They were made in God's image.

4. What relationship did God plan for there to be between these characters and the rest of His creation?

    Humans were made to rule over the rest of God's creation.

> **SUMMARY** God created mankind, and He blessed them to both rule and fill the earth. This blessing, along with land and seed (offspring), was the good gift of God to mankind. God wove these themes throughout His story of the world.

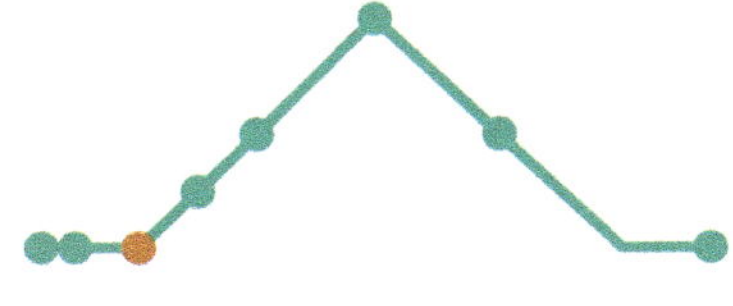

CONFLICT
Genesis 3:14–19

5. What specific conflict is mentioned that came into God's story through mankind's sin? (3:15)

The seed, or offspring, of the woman would be against the seed of the serpent.

6. Who did God plan would win the conflict?

the seed of the woman

> **SUMMARY**
> Every aspect of what God had given to mankind was affected by sin. Their rule was twisted, the land was cursed, bearing seed would be painful, and the blessed relationship with God was lost.

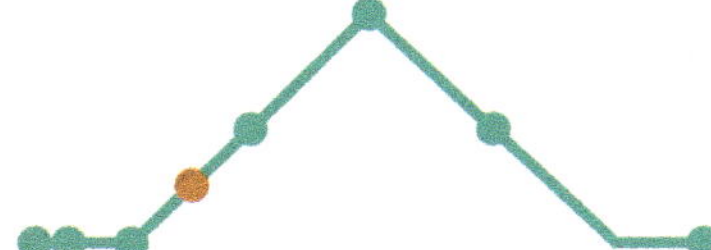

RESOLUTION FORESHADOWING
Isaiah 52:13–53:12

7. What does God say would eventually happen to His Servant? (52:13)

He would be exalted.

8. What will God's righteous Servant do in God's plan? (53:11)

He will justify many by bearing their iniquities.

> **SUMMARY**
> God had a plan in place to restore the blessing of His relationship to many people by placing the penalty of sin on His Servant.

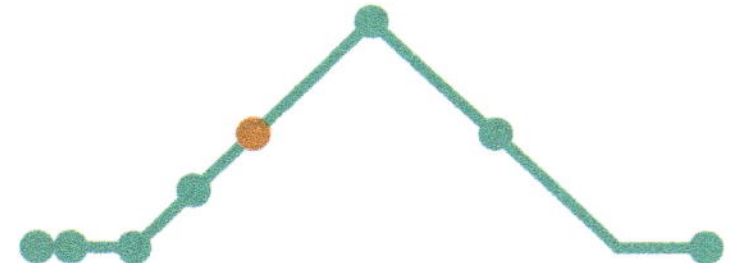

RISING ACTION
Genesis 12:1–3

9. Whom did God include in His plans for blessing?

Abram, his family, those who blessed Abram, and all families of the earth

Genesis 17:6

10. What did God promise to Abraham to show that He was in control of restoring mankind's fallen rule in His kingdom?

Kings would come from Abraham.

Exodus 19:3–6

11. What role that helps people connect with God was Israel to be a kingdom of?

priests

Basics for a Biblical Worldview

2 Samuel 7:8–13, 16

12. What did God promise to David to show that He was in control of restoring mankind's fallen rule in His kingdom?

God would establish the kingdom and throne of David's seed forever.

Jeremiah 31:31, 33–34

13. What did God promise to make with the houses of Israel and Judah?

a new covenant

14. How would the New Covenant restore the relationship between God and those who would become His people?

God will put His law in people's hearts. They will know God. God will forgive them and will not remember their sin anymore.

Ezekiel 36:24–28

15. What would be the results of this work of God in His people?

They will be cleansed. They will have new hearts and God's Spirit. They will be able to obey God. They will dwell in their fathers' land.

> **SUMMARY**
> God began using a particular family and nation to reestablish His good gifts of land, seed, and blessing and to reestablish mankind's rule in His kingdom.

CLIMAX

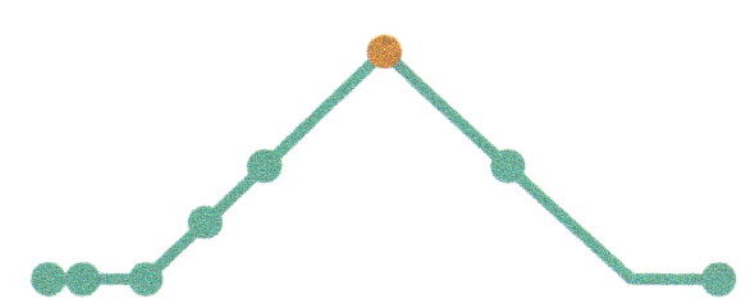

Luke 24:25–27, 44–47

16. Which events did Jesus say were the main fulfillment of all the Old Testament prophecies about the Christ (the Messiah)?

His death and resurrection (entering His glory)

1 Peter 1:18–21

17. Who was known before the world began?

Christ

18. How much of this redemption did God plan ahead of time?

all of it

> **SUMMARY**
> God brought the pieces of His plan together in the person of Jesus Christ in order to redeem the world back to Himself.

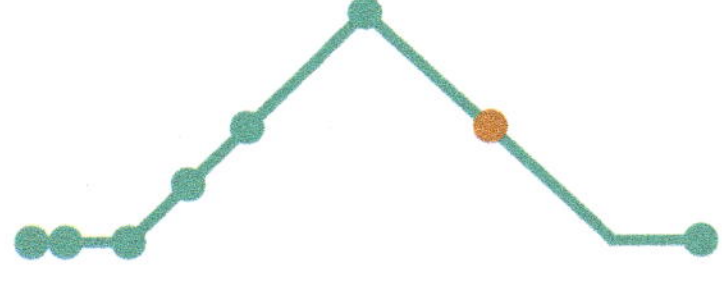

FALLING ACTION

Ephesians 1:4

19. When did God plan for New Testament believers to be part of His story?

before the foundation of the world

Matthew 16:18

20. What did Jesus promise about the church and its enemy, hell?

He would build the church, and the gates of hell would not prevail against it.

SUMMARY

God is currently restoring people back to Himself through the church and preparing them to rule well in His world when it is restored to perfection.

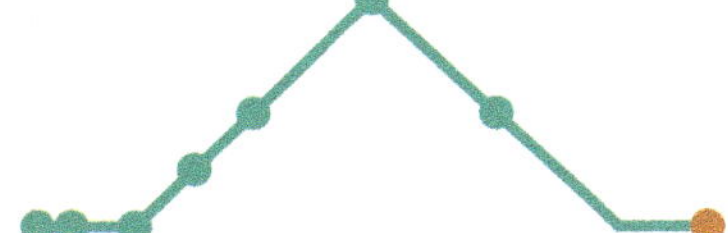

RESOLUTION

Matthew 25:34

21. What will be restored from the original creation?

mankind's rule in God's kingdom

22. When was the kingdom planned as the end of God's story?

before the foundation of the world

John 17:24

23. What is Jesus' will for His followers at the end of the story?

that they be with Him to see His glory given to Him by the Father

Revelation 20:11–15

24. What end did God plan for those whose names are not written in the Book of Life?

the lake of fire

Revelation 21:1–3

25. What did God plan for the final home of His people?

the new earth

26. What did God plan for His final relationship with His people?

He will dwell with them and be their God.

SUMMARY

God will one day restore the heavens and the earth and restore His people's relationship to Him eternally.

Basics for a Biblical Worldview

God created everything good. Much of that goodness can still be seen and understood in spite of the curse of sin that twists everything. You learned that this original goodness of God's creation is called structure. The Bible can help you understand the structure of many categories.

Read the verses and answer the questions. At the end of each category, use the truths from the verses to summarize the structure God created.

FAMILY

Genesis 2:18–24

1. What is the basic social unit that God created in this account?

   marriage

2. Why did God give the woman to the man?

   to be an appropriate helper for him

3. How is the relationship within this basic social unit described?

   The husband and wife are one flesh.

Matthew 19:6

4. Because of the relationship between husband and wife, what is their responsibility to each other?

   They are to remain together as one flesh because God joined them together that way.

Ephesians 5:22–33

5. What actions are structural in marriage?

   wives submitting to their husbands as unto the Lord; husbands loving their wives as Christ loves the church; husbands nourishing and cherishing their wives as their own bodies

6. What does Paul say that the relationship between husband and wife represents?

   the relationship between Christ and the church

Genesis 1:28

7. What would be added to the basic social unit when the Creation Mandate was obeyed?

   children [Note: Students may need clarification that the inability of some couples to have children, though they desire to, is a result of the curse.]

Deuteronomy 6:6–7

8. What responsibility do parents have toward their children?

   They are to teach God's commands to their children in all aspects of daily life.

Exodus 20:12

9. What responsibility do children have toward their parents?

   They are to honor their parents.

Proverbs 6:20

10. What responsibility do children have toward their parents' teaching?

    They are to keep their parents' commands and not forsake them.

SUMMARY

A family is a husband, wife, and children. In marriage, the husband and wife are one flesh and should not be broken apart. Wives are to submit to their husbands, and husbands are to love their wives. They represent the church and Christ in this way. They are to have children and to teach them about God. Children are to honor their parents and obey their commands.

SCHOOL

Luke 2:52

11. What did Jesus increase in as a boy?

    wisdom, stature, and favor with God and man

12. Based on how Jesus grew, what is God's created structure for how children should mature?

    God designed for children to increase in wisdom, stature, and favor with God and man as they get older.

Deuteronomy 6:6–7

13. Whom did God command to help children in their instruction?

    parents

Proverbs 1:7

14. What did God plan for instruction to start with?

    the fear of the Lord

Proverbs 4:10–14

15. How is good instruction "life"?

    It protects us from physical and spiritual dangers that threaten our lives.

16. What should a student's response be to verse 13?

    A student should get instruction through school and not let go of it.

2 Timothy 3:15–16

17. What is the source for instruction in righteousness?

    all Scripture

18. How should school subjects be based on instruction in righteousness?

    Scripture should guide the purpose and perspective of all subjects and should itself be

    taught through all the school subjects.

SUMMARY

Like Jesus grew and learned, children are to increase in wisdom and favor with God and man. School should support that goal, and parents should be helping children in their instruction. Instruction in school should begin with the fear of the Lord. School is important because it helps protect children's lives physically and spiritually. The Bible is the source for instruction and should guide the purpose and perspective of school instruction.

WORK

Genesis 1:28; 2:15

19. What work did God give humans in the beginning? What specific job did God give Adam and Eve?

    to subdue the earth and have dominion over it; to dress (tend) and keep the garden

20. Based on the information from these verses, is work a result of the curse or part of God's created structure?

It is part of God's created structure.

Nehemiah 4:1–6

21. Did the people of Jerusalem have a structural view of work? Explain.

Yes, they had a mind to work. They worked together. They kept going even though their enemies were making fun of them.

Colossians 3:23–24

22. What is the result of work?

a reward of inheritance from the Lord

Psalm 90:17

23. To whom does the psalmist look for help with work?

the Lord

Proverbs 24:27

24. Which is the first goal of work, steady income or personal comfort?

steady income

2 Thessalonians 3:10–12

25. What did Paul command the Thessalonians about work?

If anyone refused to work, he should not eat. People should work for their own food.

SUMMARY

God created work to be good. God commanded humans to work at subduing the earth and having dominion over it. Knowing God's purpose for work allows us to work with a good attitude. Work brings rewards from God, but it is also dependent on God's help. Work is the primary means of providing income and a secondary means of providing comfort. It is required in order to eat.

Creation, Fall, Redemption Timeline: Place a short description of the created structure of family, school, and work at the Creation point.

The Fall has affected every area of life. God created His world to function in a certain way, but the Fall bent that structure away from the way God designed it. Looking around at the world, you can see evidence of fallen direction in everyone's lives in one way or another.

Read the summaries of God's created structure for each category. Answer the questions about how fallen people bend structure in a fallen direction. At the end of each category, summarize the fallen direction. *Answers will vary.*

FAMILY

God created Adam and Eve to be married, to be one flesh as husband and wife. He commands couples to be fruitful and multiply by having children. He wants them to teach their children His ways. God designed a husband's love for his wife to represent God's love for His people, and a wife's submission to her husband to represent the submission of God's people to Him. God desires for children to honor their parents and obey their commands.

1. How have marriage between a man and a woman and the concept of being one flesh been twisted by the Fall?

   Many men and women practice homosexuality. Many men and women live together without getting married. Many men and women get married and then divorce even though they are supposed to be one flesh. Many have been unfaithful to their spouse.

2. How has God's command to be fruitful and multiply been twisted by the Fall?

   Because of the curse, many couples do not have the ability to bear children. Many couples refuse to have children. Many believe that couples should not have many children and that they have the right to kill unborn babies that they do not want.

3. How has God's desire for parents to teach their children His ways been twisted by the Fall?

   Many parents do not know God and cannot teach their children about Him. Many parents have rebelled against God and teach their children to do the same. Many parents abuse their children, and their children become bitter against God.

4. How has God's design for the roles of a husband and a wife been twisted by the Fall? (Genesis 3:16; 2 Timothy 3:2)

   Many men do not love their wives but love themselves instead. Many men live in a way that their wives are unable to submit to them (such as an abusive relationship). Many women refuse to submit to their husbands at all.

5. How has God's desire for children to honor and obey their parents been twisted by the Fall?

Many children do not respect their parents. Many children disobey their parents.

SCHOOL

Jesus' example of growing and learning shows that God wants children to be taught in a godly way by godly adults. Like Jesus, children are to increase in wisdom and favor with God and man. School should support that goal, and parents should be helping children in their instruction. Instruction in school should begin with the fear of the Lord. School is important because it helps protect children's lives physically and spiritually. The Bible should guide the purpose and perspective of school instruction.

6. How has the structure of children being taught by godly adults in a godly way been twisted by the Fall? (Judges 2:10–12)

Many schools are not designed to teach about God at all. Many adults are not believers in God and cannot teach students to follow God. Many things taught in schools contradict the Bible and the truths about God.

7. How have children's growth in wisdom and favor with God and man been twisted by the Fall?

Many children do not seek to grow in wisdom or in favor with God. Many seek their own way and ignore their relationship to God and other people.

8. How has the truth that wisdom and instruction begin with the fear of the Lord been twisted by the Fall?

Many schools and parents do not teach the fear of the Lord and try to teach truth without

teaching about God. Students end up without true wisdom and knowledge because they do

not first fear God.

9. Proverbs 4:13 says that good instruction is life. How have people's responses to good instruction been twisted by the Fall?

Many people do not recognize the dangers that threaten their lives, so they do not seek

good instruction as protection. Many people think they know all they need to know. Many

children have a bad attitude toward instruction and even rebel against it.

SUMMARY

Many teachers and parents are not godly and do not teach in a godly way. Teachers and

parents teach children that there is no God or that they do not need to know Him. Teachers

and parents attempt to teach without God's wisdom or the Bible. Students refuse to seek

instruction and even rebel against it.

WORK

God created work to be good. God commands humans to work at subduing the earth and having dominion over it. Knowing God's purpose for work allows people to work with a good attitude. Work brings rewards, but it is also dependent on God's help. Work is the primary means of providing income and a secondary means of providing comfort. God says that work is required in order to eat.

10. How has people's understanding of work as a created structure been twisted by the Fall?

Many people think work is a "necessary evil" and not something given to us by God. Many

people think life would be better without work and make it their goal to work as little as

possible.

11. How has working with the right attitude been twisted by the Fall?

Many people selfishly want to do their own thing and resent work because they have to do what others tell them to do. Many people have a poor attitude about work and complain about their jobs and their bosses.

12. How has dependency on God for help in work been twisted by the Fall?

Many workers do their work in their own strength, never looking to God for help. Many workers think they have their jobs and their skills because of their own doing and do not acknowledge God's gifts to them.

13. How has working for income to provide one's needs before personal comfort been twisted by the Fall?

Many people live only for their own comfort and fail to provide for their family's real needs. Many struggle to have what they need because they do not want to spend the time at work to earn the things they need.

14. How has the requirement of work for eating been twisted by the Fall?

Many people want to have food without working for it. Many want others to provide for them instead of providing for themselves when they are capable of working.

SUMMARY

Many people do not think work is a good gift from God. Workers do their jobs with a bad attitude. They do not depend on God to do good work. People try to get as much personal comfort as possible without earning what they need to get it. People want their needs to be provided for without having to work.

Creation, Fall, Redemption Timeline: Place a description of fallen direction at the point of the Fall.

Basics for a Biblical Worldview

SEEING CHRIST IN THE BIBLE'S STORY

In Section 2.5 you learned several titles given to the Hero of God's story because of the roles He played. You will see how these roles are developed with more and more information throughout the Bible.

Read the verses and answer the questions.

SEED OF THE WOMAN
Genesis 3:14–15

1. In the curse on the serpent, what did God promise about the Seed of the woman and the serpent?

   The serpent would bruise the heel of the Seed of the woman. The Seed of the woman would bruise the head of the serpent.

Genesis 8:20–22

2. What did God promise to Noah that He would not do again?

   curse the ground and destroy every living thing

3. What would continue while the earth remains?

   seedtime and harvest, cold and heat, summer and winter, and day and night

4. How will the promised stability of the world help the coming of the Seed of the woman?

   God could work through the coming generations to bring the Seed of the woman without another global disruption of the lives of humans.

Genesis 12:1–3

5. What clause shows that God was promising to Abraham (Abram) a seed, or offspring?

   "I will make of thee a great nation."

6. What did God promise about all families of the earth?

   They would all be blessed through Abraham.

7. How could the original promise about the Seed of the woman possibly connect with God's promise to bless all families of the earth through Abraham?

The Seed of the woman bruising the head of the the serpent would make it possible for all

families of the earth to be blessed. [Note: If students struggle to describe the basic

connection, encourage them to look back over the explanation in Section 2.5.]

8. Based on these promises, the Seed of the woman would also be the seed of whom?

Abraham

2 Samuel 7:12–16

9. What did God promise to David about his seed?

He would set up David's seed, establish his kingdom, and establish the throne of his

kingdom forever.

10. How could the original promise about the Seed of the woman possibly connect with God's promise to give David an eternal King on his throne? (1 Corinthians 15:24–25)

By bruising the head of the serpent, the Seed of the woman would establish his authority

as the eternal King.

11. Based on these promises, the Seed of the woman would also be the seed of whom?

David

12. God promised a Seed to Abraham and David as fathers, but He also promised a Seed to a woman, a virgin. When was a child born to a woman without a husband to fulfill this promise?

when Jesus was born to the virgin Mary

REDEEMER
Romans 5:6–8

13. In whose place did Christ die?

the ungodly, sinners

14. What did Christ's death prove, or demonstrate?

God's love for us

Galatians 3:7–14, 16

15. How did Christ make redemption from the curse of the law possible?

He was made a curse for us (He died in our place).

Basics for a Biblical Worldview

16. What promise does Christ's death make possible?

receiving the Spirit [Note: The Spirit is part of the New Covenant promises (Ezekiel 36:27).]

17. How do people receive this promise?

through faith

18. How do verses 14 and 16 show that God's promises to Abraham were fulfilled?

Verse 14 says that the blessing of Abraham for the Gentiles came about by the redemption

offered through Christ. Verse 16 says the seed promised to Abraham was Christ.

2 Corinthians 5:18–21

19. What did God do for us by Jesus Christ?

He reconciled us to Himself.

20. What did God make Christ on our behalf?

to be sin

21. How was Christ righteous?

He knew no sin (He had never sinned).

22. What are we made when we are "in" Christ?

the righteousness of God

SECOND ADAM
1 Corinthians 15:45–49

23. What did the Second (last) Adam become?

a quickening (life-giving) spirit

24. Where was the Second Adam from?

heaven

25. Based on your answers above, who is the Second Adam?

Christ

26. Whose image will believers bear, just as they bore the image of Adam?

the image of Christ

THE CHURCH'S HOPE IN TRIALS

What do you do when you face hard times? If you are a believer, it is important for you to consider your role in God's plan of redemption to help you face trials and temptations. Believers throughout history have found that God in His wisdom places them in difficult circumstances where they can use their hope to point others to Him.

Read the verses and answer the questions. At the end, summarize the church's role in God's plan of redemption while they are suffering.

1 Peter 1:3–9

1. How has God given believers a living hope?

   by Jesus Christ's resurrection

2. What keeps believers until the revelation of full salvation?

   the power of God

3. What can bring heaviness, or grief, to believers?

   temptations or trials

4. What is the result of the testing of believers' faith?

   praise and honor and glory when Jesus Christ appears (is revealed)

5. Based on these verses, how can believers have hope in trials?

   They know God has saved them and keeps them for their inheritance in heaven. Their faith during trials will result in praise, honor, and glory to Jesus when they see Him and their salvation is complete. Their faith in Him gives them joy in the meantime.

1 Peter 2:11–15

6. What does Peter urge believers to avoid?

   fleshly lusts

7. What will result from their good response to unbelievers' accusations?

   Unbelievers will see the believers' good works and glorify God.

8. For whose sake do believers obey those in authority?

   the Lord's

9. What effect will believers' good works have on foolish men?

   They will silence the foolish men's ignorance.

10. Who is the believer's example of suffering for doing right?

    Christ

11. How did Christ endure when He was treated so badly though He was innocent?

    He refused to revile (insult) or try to hurt those who persecuted Him. He committed Himself

    to His Father who would judge righteously.

1 Peter 3:14–17

12. Instead of being afraid of what people might say, what should every believer be ready with?

    an answer (defense) for those who ask for the reason that the believer has hope

13. What causes unbelievers to be ashamed after they accuse believers?

    The believers actually have a good conscience and good behavior in Christ.

14. What does Peter say about suffering for doing wrong? Why?

    It is better to suffer for doing good than for doing wrong. Suffering for doing wrong does not

    help unbelievers understand and desire the believer's hope.

15. Whom is God using to spread His message of hope?

    believers (the church)

SUMMARY

Believers are to avoid sin and do good so that unbelievers will give glory to God and fools

will be silenced. Believers should reflect Christ by suffering for doing right as He did. Believers

should speak of their hope from God and live so that it cannot be spoken against.

Creation, Fall, Redemption Timeline: Place the church age (beginning with Pentecost up to the present) on your timeline. Place yourself on the timeline with a description of the believer's redemptive responsibilities during suffering from your summary above.

GOD'S PLAN OF RESTORATION

In Section 2.6 you learned that God has a plan to redeem His people from the physical results of the Fall. The following verses speak of God's full redemption which will restore all things through Christ's resurrection.

Read the verses and answer the questions.

1 Corinthians 15:20–26, 42–49

1. How is Christ's resurrection the first taste of full redemption?

   Believers will be resurrected from the dead like Christ.

2. When will this full redemption of believers happen?

   when Christ comes

3. How will Christ restore God's full, righteous dominion over the earth?

   He will deliver up the kingdom to the Father by putting down all ruling enemies.

4. What is the last enemy of full redemption?

   death

5. How do verses 42–43 describe the fallen, natural body?

   corrupt, dishonorable, and weak

6. How are these three problems contrasted in the new redeemed body?

   The new redeemed body is incorruptible, glorious, and powerful.

7. Whose image will believers' bodies bear?

   the heavenly man's, Christ's

Creation, Fall, Redemption Timeline: Full restoration will take place only when Christ returns. Place the second coming of Christ at an unknown point in the near future. Include a description of Christ's restoration of believers and the rest of creation (Romans 8:18–23; Revelation 21:1–4).

Analyze this chart, which describes the Creation, Fall, and Redemption of three categories: the image of God, the Creation Mandate, and mankind's relationship with God. Read the verses and complete the chart with redemptive direction.

Image of God

Creational Structure	**Genesis 1:27** Mankind was made like God.
Fallen Direction	**Genesis 4:8** Mankind became sinful, selfish, and rebellious against God.
Redemptive Direction	**Romans 8:29; 1 John 2:2** *God is conforming believers to the image of Christ.*

Creation Mandate

Creational Structure	**Genesis 1:28** Mankind was given dominion over the earth.
Fallen Direction	**Genesis 4:16–17** Mankind attempted dominion selfishly and independently of God.
Redemptive Direction	**Revelation 11:15; 22:3–5** *Christ will fulfill the Creation Mandate by ruling with His servants forever.*

Relationship with God

Creational Structure	**Genesis 3:8** Mankind had a perfect relationship with God.
Fallen Direction	**Isaiah 59:2** Mankind was separated from God by sin.
Redemptive Direction	**2 Corinthians 5:17–19** *God has reconciled believers to Himself in Christ.*

Basics for a Biblical Worldview

"FOLLOW YOUR HEART"

Popular people say a lot of things that their fans quote as great wisdom. How can you tell what's really wise or not? Figuring out which ideas are right or wrong is what discernment is all about. You have to discern what is God's structure for creation and where people have bent that in a fallen direction. Here are some of those quotations for you to check against the Bible for fallen direction.

Read the quotations and use the verses to answer the questions with biblical discernment.

TRUST YOUR OWN INSTINCTS, GO INSIDE, FOLLOW YOUR HEART. RIGHT FROM THE START, GO AHEAD AND STAND UP FOR WHAT YOU BELIEVE IN. AS I'VE LEARNED, THAT'S THE PATH TO HAPPINESS.

—LESLEY ANN WARREN, AMERICAN ACTRESS

Jeremiah 17:9

1. If your beliefs are based on your own heart, will they be based on truth? Explain.

   No, since my heart is deceitful, it will not tell me the truth.

Proverbs 28:26

2. Proverbs uses just one word to describe the inner being of a person, including both the heart and mind. According to this verse, why should you not trust your heart-mind?

   The one who trusts in his own heart-mind is a fool.

I ALWAYS BELIEVED THAT WHEN YOU FOLLOW YOUR HEART OR YOUR GUT, WHEN YOU REALLY FOLLOW THE THINGS THAT FEEL GREAT TO YOU, YOU CAN NEVER LOSE, BECAUSE SETTLING IS THE WORST FEELING IN THE WORLD.

—RIHANNA, BARBADIAN SINGER-SONGWRITER

Ecclesiastes 9:3

3. What is the problem with following "things that feel great to you"?

   The heart is so full of evil that the things that feel great may truly be wrong.

4. Why is it not true that if you follow your heart you cannot lose?

The way that seems right to people actually ends in death.

YOUR HEART AND YOUR INSTINCTS ARE FAR MORE RELIABLE THAN YOUR BRAIN. WHEN YOU FOLLOW YOUR HEART, YOU CAN BE SURE YOU WON'T REGRET IT LATER. EVEN IF YOU CALCULATE YOUR EVERY MOVE, IT'S NOT LIKE LIFE EVER GOES ACCORDING TO PLAN.

—NITHYA MENEN, INDIAN ACTRESS

Proverbs 12:8

5. Here again, Proverbs uses one word for the heart-mind. According to this verse, what is the real difference between the ways a person could use his heart-mind?

A person could use his heart-mind to live wisely and give wisdom to others. Or, a person could use his heart-mind for twisted, sinful living.

James 1:14–15

6. Why is it not true that you won't regret following your heart?

My evil desires will tempt me to sin, and the consequence of sin is death.

I'M HERE TO SPREAD A MESSAGE OF HOPE. FOLLOW YOUR HEART. DON'T FOLLOW WHAT YOU'VE BEEN TOLD YOU'RE SUPPOSED TO DO.

—J. COLE, AMERICAN RAPPER

Proverbs 12:15

7. Why should you not follow your heart but instead follow the things you've been told?

It is foolish to follow your own way. It is wise to listen to advice, especially when the advice is truth from the Lord.

Proverbs 19:21

8. What will actually stand, or be accomplished?

the Lord's counsel

MAKE SURE THAT YOU ALWAYS FOLLOW YOUR HEART AND YOUR GUT, AND LET YOURSELF BE WHO YOU WANT TO BE, AND WHO YOU KNOW YOU ARE. AND DON'T LET ANYONE STEAL YOUR JOY.

—JONATHAN GROFF, AMERICAN ACTOR

Matthew 15:18–19

9. How is it a problem to "be who you want to be"?

   My heart is full of evil. If I let myself be who my heart wants me to be, the result will be evil.

Habakkuk 3:17–18

10. What does Jonathan Groff imply is the source of your joy?

    following your heart and being yourself

11. What do these verses say should be the source of your joy?

    the Lord, the God of my salvation

FAITH THAT IT'S NOT ALWAYS IN YOUR HANDS OR THINGS DON'T ALWAYS GO THE WAY YOU PLANNED, BUT YOU HAVE TO HAVE FAITH THAT THERE IS A PLAN FOR YOU, AND YOU MUST FOLLOW YOUR HEART AND BELIEVE IN YOURSELF NO MATTER WHAT.

—MARTINA MCBRIDE, AMERICAN SINGER-SONGWRITER

12. What word makes this quotation sound like biblical advice?

    faith

13. How do you know that Martina McBride was not using that word biblically?

    She said to believe in yourself, instead of saying to believe or have faith in God.

14. Which part of a worldview is obvious from all these quotations?

    A person's loves (in this case, love for self) drive his basic beliefs.

Read the verses and answer the questions. Summarize what the Bible says is the right alternative to following your heart.

Proverbs 3:5–6

15. How can these verses give you more confidence than the advice from the quotations?

I can trust in the Lord's plan for my life since I can't trust my own heart to plan my life. He is

leading me as I submit to Him.

Psalm 119:10–11

16. What can you do to keep your heart from leading you astray?

Seek God. Obey and meditate on God's Word.

SUMMARY

The Bible says to trust the Lord instead of my own sinful desires or thinking. I must seek Him

instead of my own way. God's Word is the source of solid truth that I can trust.

Basics for a Biblical Worldview

You have looked at both the structure and the fallen direction in family, school, and work. Now you are ready to complete this Making Connections chart with actions that people can take to push each category in a redemptive direction.

Read the verses and complete the chart.

Family	
Creational Structure	God created Adam and Eve to be married, to be one flesh as husband and wife. He commands couples to be fruitful and multiply by having children. He wants them to teach their children His ways. God designed a husband's love for his wife to represent God's love for His people, and a wife's submission to her husband to represent the submission of God's people to Him. God desires for children to honor their parents and obey their commands.
Fallen Direction	Many people disregard God's design for marriage between a man and a woman. Couples live together and refuse to get married, or they divorce once married. People refuse to have children. People fail to teach their children about God or even abuse them. Husbands refuse to love their families and rule them well. Wives refuse to submit to their husbands. Children refuse to honor and obey their parents.
Redemptive Direction	**Matthew 19:4–6** **Ephesians 5:22–33** **Deuteronomy 6:6–7** **Exodus 20:12** **Proverbs 6:20** *Husbands and wives should avoid divorce. Husbands and wives should be faithful to each other. Husbands should love their wives by sacrificing their own desires for them, and wives should submit to their husbands as to the Lord. Parents should seek to teach their children about God and His Word. Children should seek to honor and obey their parents.*

School	
Creational Structure	Jesus' example of growing and learning shows that God wants children to be taught in a godly way by godly adults. Like Jesus, children are to increase in wisdom and favor with God and man. School should support that goal, and parents should be helping children in their instruction. Instruction in school should begin with the fear of the Lord. School is important because it helps protect children's lives physically and spiritually. The Bible should guide the purpose and perspective of school instruction.
Fallen Direction	Many teachers and parents are not godly and do not teach in a godly way. Teachers and parents teach children that there is no God or that they do not need to know Him. Teachers and parents attempt to teach without God's wisdom or the Bible. Students refuse to seek instruction and even rebel against it.

Redemptive Direction	Luke 2:52 Deuteronomy 6:6–7 Proverbs 1:7 Proverbs 4:13 2 Timothy 3:15–16	*Children should use school as an opportunity to grow in wisdom and in favor with God and man. Parents should take responsibility for the godly instruction of their children. Since the fear of the Lord is the beginning of wisdom, everyone needs to repent and trust Christ for salvation in order to learn God's wisdom. Teachers should seek to teach the fear of the Lord first. Children should seek instruction as a way to guard their lives. Believers should use instruction in righteousness from the Bible throughout all school subjects.*

Work

Creational Structure	God created work to be good. God commands humans to work at subduing the earth and having dominion over it. Knowing God's purpose for work allows people to work with a good attitude. Work brings rewards, but it is also dependent on God's help. Work is the primary means of providing income and a secondary means of providing comfort. God says that work is required in order to eat.
Fallen Direction	Many people do not think work is a good gift from God. Workers do their jobs with a bad attitude. They do not depend on God to do good work. People try to get as much personal comfort as possible without earning what they need to get it. People want their needs to be provided for without having to work.

Redemptive Direction	Genesis 1:28 Nehemiah 4:6 Colossians 3:23–24 Proverbs 24:27 2 Thessalonians 3:10	*Everyone should seek to see work as a gift from God in His very good creation. Workers should have a good attitude toward work. Workers should look to the Lord for help with their work and work with God's rewards in mind. Workers should earn income to provide for their needs before comfort. Everyone should work before feeling entitled to eat.*

Basics for a Biblical Worldview

Read the verses and answer the questions.

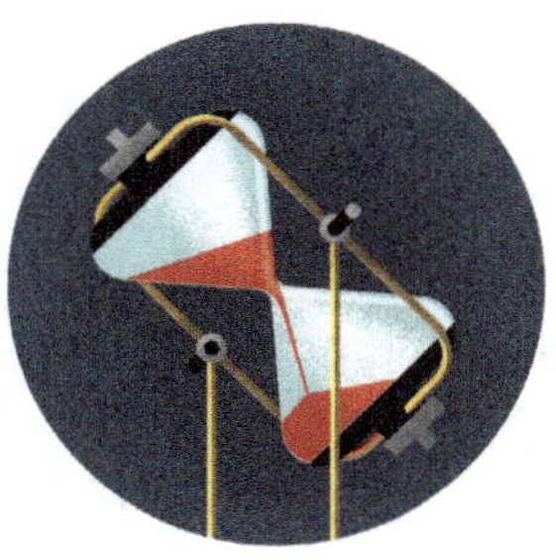

ETERNAL
Psalm 90:2

1. How does this verse demonstrate that God is eternal?

   He is God from everlasting to everlasting. His existence is not dependent on the created world or time.

UNCHANGING
Malachi 3:5–6

2. How do God's people see His unchanging nature in action?

   God does not completely destroy His people when He punishes them for their sin. He keeps His word.

ALL-POWERFUL (OMNIPOTENT)
Revelation 1:8

3. How does this verse demonstrate that God is omnipotent?

   He is called the Almighty.

Luke 1:37

4. Why do you need to know this truth from God about His promises?

   I might be tempted to think that God's promises are impossible for Him to fulfill.

PRESENT EVERYWHERE (OMNIPRESENT)
Acts 17:27–28

5. How does this verse demonstrate that God is omnipresent?

   God is not far away from us; all of us live and move and have our being in Him.

Psalm 139:7–10

6. What question did the psalmist use to show that God is omnipresent?

   Where can I run away from your presence (or Spirit)?

7. What extremes did the psalmist use to show God's omnipresence?

heaven and hell (Sheol); the place where the morning begins and the farthest parts of the

sea [Note: For those living in Israel, these opposites represented the east and the west.]

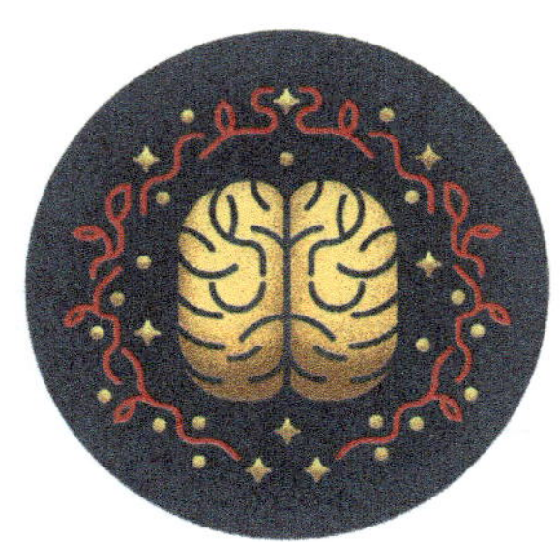

ALL-KNOWING (OMNISCIENT)
Psalm 139:4

8. How does this verse demonstrate that God is omniscient?

He knows every word of ours, even those we are just about to say.

1 Samuel 16:7

9. How did God explain to Samuel that He is omniscient?

Samuel could only look on the outward appearance of a person, but God can actually see

and know what is in a person's heart.

THE TRINITY
Matthew 28:19

10. What singular and plural contrast in this verse demonstrates the *tri-unity* of God?

The verse mentions a singular "name," but three persons are listed: the Father, the Son, and

the Holy Spirit. This contrast demonstrates three persons, one God.

John 1:1–3

11. How do these verses show the Word to be God, one of the persons of the Trinity?

The Word (Jesus) already existed in the beginning and was God. He also made all things—

another fact that demonstrates His divine nature.

Acts 5:3–4

12. How do these verses show the Holy Spirit to be God, one of the persons of the Trinity?

Peter said that Ananias lied to the Holy Spirit and later said that he lied to God (speaking

of the same lie).

Basics for a Biblical Worldview

What is truth? Philosophy has always tried to answer this question. Too often, however, unbelieving philosophers seek truth while denying God and His place as Creator and sustainer of the world. Since the fear of the Lord is the beginning of wisdom, these philosophers cannot actually begin to define *truth*. Section 3.2 explained that truth is *reality as interpreted by God*. Because God is the source of truth, you will learn about God Himself as you learn about truth. You will identify the connections the Bible makes between truth and God's own nature and actions.

Read the verses and complete the chart.

	What I Learn about Truth	**What I Learn about God**
John 17:15–17	*Truth makes God's people sanctified while they are in the world. Truth is God's Word.*	God is the source of truth.
Psalm 119:89	*Truth is eternal.*	God's Word is eternal.
Titus 1:2	Truth is the only thing God speaks, which includes His promises for the future.	*God cannot lie.*
John 17:3	I can know truth.	*I can know God.*
John 14:6	*The truth is found in Jesus.*	*Jesus is God and the only way to God.*
John 1:14	The fullest display of truth in a human is Jesus.	*Jesus can be full of truth because He is God.*
John 14:16–17	Truth continues to be known through the Holy Spirit after Jesus' ascension. The world rejects truth.	*The Spirit of truth dwells in those who know Him (believers).*
1 John 5:6	*The truth about Jesus' coming is confirmed by the Spirit.*	The Holy Spirit's job is to bear witness, or testify, about Jesus.

Use the completed chart to summarize two things: a definition of _truth_ and the connections between truth and God's nature and actions.

SUMMARY

Truth can be known through God's eternal revelation. Truth is what God gives in His Word, including what He speaks and what He promises. We also know truth through Jesus and the Holy Spirit's witness.

SUMMARY

God speaks truth, and He cannot lie. Truth is part of the nature of God; therefore, His Word is truth. Truth is eternal because it comes from God, who is eternal. God embodies truth in the person of Jesus Christ and allows truth to dwell in believers through the Holy Spirit.

Basics for a Biblical Worldview

You should recognize from Section 3.3 that God has built into each person a sense of what is good and what is evil. You should also understand that because of our fallen nature, we still need God to give us a true standard of what is good. This is the standard of good from above.

Read the verses and answer the questions. At the end of each category, use the truths from the verses to summarize a definition.

GOOD

Psalm 100:5

1. Who is the ultimate standard of good?

   the Lord

2. How is this goodness demonstrated toward humans?

   The Lord's mercy (love) and truth (faithfulness) keep going forever.

Nehemiah 9:13

3. What is described as good?

   God's statutes and commandments

4. How do the truths from this verse and Psalm 100:5 connect to each other?

   Because God is good, His commandments are good as well.

Matthew 22:37–39

5. How do the truths from these verses and Nehemiah 9:13 connect to each other?

   Because God's commandments are good, it is good to love God and love others.

Luke 10:38–42

6. What did Jesus affirm was good?

   sitting at His feet to hear Him

7. What did Jesus imply was not good?

   being worried about things not so important

8. How do the truths from these verses and Matthew 22:37–39 connect to each other?

Because loving God is a good commandment, it was good for Mary to show her love for God by listening to Jesus.

Psalm 73:28

9. What is described as good?

to draw near to God

10. How did Mary follow the truth of this psalm in Luke 10:38–42?

Mary chose the good thing by drawing near to God in the person of Jesus Christ.

Romans 7:7–12

11. What was God's good law designed to bring?

life

12. Why did the law fail to bring this?

As sinners, we cannot keep the law.

13. What did the law teach Paul?

what sin was

Lamentations 3:26

14. What is described as good?

to hope and wait for the salvation of the Lord

15. How does this verse give the solution to the problem in Romans 7:7–12?

Only God can save us from our sin.

SUMMARY

Good is what reflects God's character. Because the law shows God's character, obedience to the law is good. People are not good like God because they sin. People can be good only when they have been saved and learn goodness from Jesus, who shows the character of God in human form.

Basics for a Biblical Worldview

EVIL

James 1:13

16. In what ways is God separate from evil?

    He cannot be tempted with evil, nor does He ever tempt anyone to evil.

Mark 7:20–23

17. Where does evil dwell?

    in the heart of a person

18. How do evil actions come from the heart?

    Evil actions begin with some thought or decision in the heart. [Note: Students may also answer that the heart is another way of describing the flesh, or sin nature.]

19. What things did Jesus say are evil?

    evil thoughts, adulteries, fornications (sexual immorality), murders, thefts, covetousness, wickedness, deceit, lasciviousness (sensuality), an evil eye (envy), blasphemy (slander), pride, and foolishness

1 Timothy 6:10

20. How is the love of money the root of all kinds of evil?

    The love of money keeps people from faith in the gospel and brings many sorrows.

Hebrews 3:12

21. What is evidence of an evil heart?

    unbelief and trying to get away from God

SUMMARY

Anything that is contrary to God and His law is evil. Because people's hearts are evil and thus separated from God, the things people's hearts seek to do (outside the control of the Holy Spirit) are also evil.

In Section 3.4 you learned that God Himself is beautiful (Psalm 27:4). God's beauty includes His moral perfection. In other words, His moral perfection is the ultimate expression of beauty.

Not only is God beautiful, but He also created beautiful things. All that is beautiful received its beauty from Him. Though the Bible talks about beauty, it doesn't give us a complete definition. We discern what is beautiful according to the order of creation around us and according to God's moral perfection.

Based on the work of many non-Christian and Christian writers over many centuries, Bible teacher R. C. Sproul describes how to discern created order in the arts. He gives four basic principles.

1 PROPORTION

A composition with proportion presents objects or parts of an object as how they truly are in relation to each other. If you've ever tried to draw people, you know that proportion can be difficult to get right. Music and writing must balance tension with resolution.

2 HARMONY

Certain musical tones fit well together. Certain colors work well together. Poets use literary devices to create harmony in a line or stanza. A composition has harmony when all the pieces work together to make the whole better.

3 SIMPLICITY

A carefully written melody need not be complicated to be beautiful all by itself. A simple line in a painting can elegantly depict the form of something. The best stories include simple language to help the reader understand the meaning.

4 COMPLEXITY

Together, simple melodies played on different instruments can create a great musical composition. Paintings with multiple colors and layers create interest and depth. Complexity means that simple parts have been purposefully brought together.

These principles have been masterfully created by God and are His gifts to mankind. Since God made us in His image, we have the ability to appreciate beauty—whether or not we know all the details or terms for describing it.

We're all pleased by a well-written story, meticulously crafted art, the flawless performance of a master musician, or even tasteful furniture arranged by an interior designer. All these things show the handiwork of the artist and are considered beautiful.

Does this mean that everything humans make is beautiful? Or can God's gifts of order be corrupted? Certainly, something evil can be twisted to seem beautiful (Genesis 3:1–6). But only when art, music, design, and literature reflect the order and moral perfections of God can they be truly beautiful.

What about physical beauty? The Bible acknowledges the beauty of human beings. Some may be remarkably pleasing, but every person has a unique beauty (Psalm 139:14) because each one is made in God's image. A Christian also has inner beauty—spiritual qualities that reflect God's character. This beauty increases the more Christians seek God's will and purposes for their lives.

1. Where does beauty originate? (Psalm 27:4; Genesis 2:9)

   with God, who is beautiful Himself

2. Why are we able to appreciate beauty? (Genesis 1:26–27)

   We are made in God's image.

3. How can we make things that are beautiful?

   by conforming the things we make to God's order in creation and to His moral perfection

4. What are four principles of beauty?

   proportion, harmony, simplicity, complexity

5. How do these four principles of beauty relate to God's creation?

   We see all four of these throughout creation.

6. How does a Christian become more beautiful?

   by developing spiritual qualities; by seeking God's will and purposes for his or her life

Remember these four principles of beauty introduced in the previous activity? You will practice evaluating paintings and musical compositions for beauty with these principles.

Proportion: All parts balanced in relationship to the whole and each other
Harmony: Various parts working together to enhance the whole
Simplicity: Clean, minimalistic design that is understandable
Complexity: Many purposeful details creating interest and depth

Examine and evaluate the following paintings using the four principles.
Answers will vary.

The Night Watch
by Rembrandt van Rijn

1. What elements of this painting contribute to its beauty?

   The light and dark colors work together in harmony to make the painting beautiful.

The Great Wave off Kanagawa
by Katsushika Hokusai

2. What elements of this painting contribute to its beauty?

   The complexity of the wave breakers alongside the simplicity of the wave shape make the painting beautiful.

The Hay Wain
by John Constable

3. What elements of this painting contribute to its beauty?

   The true proportions of the landscape, building, and people make the painting beautiful.

Composition VII
by Wassily Kandinsky

4. What element seems most distorted in this painting?

Daniel-Henry Kahnweiler
by Pablo Picasso

5. What element seems most distorted in this painting?

Reflection of the Big Dipper
by Jackson Pollock

6. What element seems most distorted in this painting?

Basics for a Biblical Worldview

Listen to and evaluate the following musical compositions using the four principles. *Answers will vary.*

"Canon in D Major"
by Johann Pachelbel

7. What elements of this composition contribute to its beauty?

The simplicity and harmony of the chords repeated throughout make the composition beautiful.

Rondo from Horn Concerto No. 4 in E-flat
by Wolfgang Amadeus Mozart

8. What elements of this composition contribute to its beauty?

The simplicity of the melody and the complexity of the parts played by different instruments besides the horn make the composition beautiful.

Finale of *Firebird Suite*
by Igor Stravinsky

9. What elements of this composition contribute to its beauty?

The complexity of the melody and the proportion of soft and loud sounds and tension and resolution make the composition beautiful.

"Wana Baraka"
(Kenyan folk song)

10. What elements of this composition contribute to its beauty?

The harmony of many tones together make the composition beautiful.

Allegro from Violin Concerto
by Alban Berg

11. What element seems most distorted in this composition?

The chords are distorted by not harmonizing. There is too much tension and no resolution.

Music for Piano
by John Cage

12. What element seems most distorted in this composition?

<u>*The melody is distorted by having no harmony or resolution. It is simple, but instead of*</u>

<u>*communicating a message, it is meaningless.*</u>

____

Basics for a Biblical Worldview

Section 3.5 helped you understand love based on who God is and what He has done. Now you also understand what His love should mean to you. Look up these verses in your own Bible or reread the portions of Section 3.5 that mention these verses as you review these concepts.

Read the verses and answer the questions.

John 3:16

1. What does this famous verse say about love?

   God showed His love for the world by giving His Son in order to give eternal life to those who believe in Him.

John 15:13

2. How did Jesus demonstrate His great love for us?

   He laid down his life for us on the cross.

Matthew 22:35–40

3. How does love for God and neighbor relate to the law?

   All the law and the prophets are based on these two commandments to love.

1 Corinthians 13:3

4. Does this verse prove that love can be completely defined as self-sacrificial giving? Explain.

   No, it states that you can give sacrificially without having love, so there must be more to love than just self-sacrificial giving.

Luke 11:42–43

5. How did the Pharisees' actions support the idea that love is "your heart going out to something"?

   The Pharisees did not show good love by having hearts that loved God, but they did show bad love with hearts that loved attention from people.

1 John 4:8

6. Who is the standard for love?

God

7. What does this verse reveal about those who do not love?

They do not know God.

1 John 4:19

8. Who first loved?

God

9. What should be our response to this love, according to the verse?

We should love as God loves.

John 17:24

10. How does this verse prove that love is eternal?

It shows that the persons of the Trinity loved each other before the foundation of the world

(before time began).

Romans 8:38–39

11. What can separate us from the love of God?

nothing

Identify each way of showing love from the verses.

Ways to Show Love	
John 3:16	*giving something precious*
John 15:13	*laying down your life*
Psalm 103:13	*pitying (having compassion on) another*
John 14:15	*keeping commandments*
Ruth 1:16	*staying with someone, being faithful*

Basics for a Biblical Worldview

Read the verses and find what works of God they are describing. Write a sentence of what God did or does for the reason given on each chart. At the end, summarize your findings into a paragraph explaining the reason for God's works.

For His Sake	
2 Kings 19:31–34	*God defends Jerusalem for His sake.*
Isaiah 43:22, 25	*God blots out and does not remember the sins of Jacob and Israel for His sake.*
Isaiah 48:10–11	*God refines Israel with affliction for His sake.*
Matthew 10:39	*God gives life to those who lose their lives for Jesus' sake.*
2 Corinthians 12:9–10	*God acts with strength for those who are weak and suffering for Christ's sake.*
Philippians 1:29	*God gives believers suffering for Christ's sake (for Him, on behalf of Christ).*

For His Name's Sake	
1 Samuel 12:22	*The Lord does not forsake His people for His name's sake.*
Psalm 23:3	*The Lord leads His people in the paths of righteousness for His name's sake.*
Psalm 106:7–8	*The Lord saved the fathers of the psalmist for His name's sake.*
Isaiah 48:9	*God defers (delays) His anger for His name's sake.*
Ezekiel 20:9	*God brought Israel out of Egypt for His name's sake.*
1 John 2:12	*God forgives believers' sins for His name's sake.*

<table>
<tr><th colspan="2">For His Praise</th></tr>
<tr><td>Psalm 40:3</td><td>God gave the psalmist a new song for His praise.</td></tr>
<tr><td>Isaiah 43:21</td><td>God formed His people for His praise.</td></tr>
<tr><td>Isaiah 48:9</td><td>God restrains His anger for His praise.</td></tr>
<tr><td>Jeremiah 13:11</td><td>God caused Israel to stay close to Him as a people for His praise.</td></tr>
<tr><td>Jeremiah 33:8–9</td><td>God cleanses His people from their sin and forgives them for His praise.</td></tr>
<tr><td>Joel 2:24–26</td><td>God will restore what He allowed to be destroyed for His praise.</td></tr>
<tr><td>Romans 15:9–11</td><td>God had mercy on the Gentiles for His praise.</td></tr>
<tr><td>Ephesians 1:5–6</td><td>God predestined us to be adopted to Himself for His praise.</td></tr>
<tr><td>Ephesians 1:13–14</td><td>The Holy Spirit seals believers and guarantees their inheritance for His praise.</td></tr>
</table>

<table>
<tr><th colspan="2">For His Glory</th></tr>
<tr><td>Psalm 102:13, 15</td><td>God will have mercy on Zion so that the kings of the earth will fear His glory.</td></tr>
<tr><td>Isaiah 43:7</td><td>God created those who are called by His name for His glory.</td></tr>
<tr><td>Isaiah 45:25</td><td>God justifies His people so that they glory in Him.</td></tr>
<tr><td>Isaiah 48:10–11</td><td>God refines His people for His exclusive glory.</td></tr>
<tr><td>Isaiah 59:18–19</td><td>God's judgment will cause people to fear His glory.</td></tr>
<tr><td>Isaiah 66:18–19</td><td>God will gather the nations to see His glory and will send some to declare it to those who have not seen it.</td></tr>
</table>

Basics for a Biblical Worldview

For His Glory (continued)

Ezekiel 39:21	*God will set His glory among the heathen (the nations) by His judgment.*
Luke 17:17–18	*Jesus healed the lepers for God's glory.*
Luke 24:26	*Christ suffered for His glory.*
John 11:4, 40–44	*God allowed Lazarus to be sick and die so that Jesus could raise him for God's glory.*
Ephesians 1:13–14	*God sealed believers with the Holy Spirit until He fully redeems them for His glory.*
Revelation 4:11	*God created all things for His glory.*

SUMMARY

Answers will vary but should include that all God's actions—in His creation, for His people, and toward unbelievers—are for His own glory, not for the sake of anyone else.

People identify themselves in many ways. After reading Section 4.1, you've probably realized the ways you do too. The Bible talks about many of these legitimate differences. However, it is quick to call out fallen direction when people make their differences the main foundation for identity, instead of submitting to God's foundation for identity.

Evaluate the following statements about identity by completing the Making Connections chart. For creational structure, describe how God created these aspects of identity to be. For fallen direction, describe how the quotation bends God's creational structure. For redemptive direction, describe how the thinking from the quotation could be pushed back toward the creational structure.

Read the verses and complete the charts.

Ethnicity	"[If black people] wish to set their eyes on a higher power and bend their knee to pray to and worship something then perhaps our own African gods are the best way to go. At least we thought of them ourselves, we worship them ourselves, we tell their stories ourselves, they are gods made by us and for us and I think that's the best it's ever going to be." —Pauline Aphiaa
Creational Structure	**Genesis 1:28; 9:1; Acts 17:26–27** *God commanded Adam and then Noah after the Flood to fill the earth. All ethnic groups are descendants of Adam and Noah. The Creator God is the God of all ethnicities, not only one.*
Fallen Direction	This woman believes that ethnicity should determine which god people worship, instead of God's revelation of Himself in the Bible.
Redemptive Direction	**Romans 3:22–23, 29** We can identify with our ethnic heritages, except for the parts within every ethnic culture that encourage us to sin. No matter what ethnic heritage we have, we all should worship the one true God and be reconciled to Him through Christ.

Citizenship (Nationality)	"For humanity in time of peace, for the fatherland [one's own country] in time of war." —Fritz Haber, about his participation in chemical warfare for Germany
Creational Structure	**Genesis 9:6; Romans 13:1–4** God created humans to respect each other individually, with no murdering. He instituted nations and governments to take care of their citizens and interact respectfully, with no unjust wars.
Fallen Direction	*By willingly participating in killing those from other nations in order to take their liberty, Haber demonstrated that his nation ruled his heart as an idol, to the point that he followed his nation into sin against God and His law.*
Redemptive Direction	**Acts 5:29; Hebrews 13:17** We must recognize that loyalty to God and His law must be our primary loyalty, above loyalty to our nation. We can work within our government to help it fulfill God's purpose for individual and national interactions.

Sports	"I'd always been the 'soccer girl.' . . . After I tore my ACL, my identity . . . [was] suddenly gone. . . . I struggled to find who I was outside of soccer. Without it, I didn't know . . . how to describe myself." —Rachel Shinnick
Creational Structure	**Colossians 2:8–10; 1 Timothy 4:8** God wants all people to have their identity in Christ first. Exercising one's body through sports has some benefit, but not nearly as much as training in Christlikeness.
Fallen Direction	*This woman allowed her whole identity to be defined by her sport instead of by Christ. When she lost her sport, she lost her identity. Outside of Christ, no identity is fully satisfying or permanent.*
Redemptive Direction	**Galatians 2:20; 1 Corinthians 10:31** In Christ, we can engage in sports without letting the identity of being an athlete take over the higher identity of being a Christian and acting for God's glory.

Basics for a Biblical Worldview

Education	"There just isn't me. Every now and then I want to play soccer, listen to music, or read a book, but when I want to do some of these things in the middle of preparing for the exams, everyone around me says, 'You're a student preparing for [university] exams, you should be studying.' So when I'm prepping for exams, who I am is just lost." —Ho Jae-woo
Creational Structure	**Genesis 1:28; Luke 2:52** God wants humans to learn and grow through education in order to subdue and have dominion, but God never intended them to lose the other aspects of their identities in education.
Fallen Direction	This young man's culture has made education an idol—so much so that students do not even know their own personal identities, which include the skills and traits that God has given them to use in ways besides studying.
Redemptive Direction	**Proverbs 12:1; 1 Corinthians 1:30** *In Christ, we can approach education correctly as a necessary part of our lives. We will recognize that Christ is an even more important source of wisdom than education.*

Work	"Perhaps long [work] hours are [a] . . . race for status and income . . . . Or maybe the logic here isn't economic at all. It's emotional—even spiritual. The best-educated and highest-earning Americans, who can have whatever they want, have chosen the office for the same reason that devout Christians attend church on Sundays: It's where they feel most themselves."
	—Derek Thompson
Creational Structure	**Genesis 2:1–3** *In the Creation week, God gave examples of both working and resting from work so that humans would do the same.*
Fallen Direction	The people described by this writer find their identity in their work—so much so that they neglect other important parts of life, including rest, to work more and more.
Redemptive Direction	**Mark 6:31** In Christ, we understand the balance of work and rest. We can work hard without making a job into our identity. We can also rest from work and recognize the importance of using our free time to build relationships and serve others.

Basics for a Biblical Worldview

Read the verses and record what the Bible describes as your identity.

CREATED IN THE IMAGE OF GOD

Genesis 1:27

1. *image-bearer of God*

Psalm 139:14

2. *fearfully and wonderfully made*

FALLEN IN ADAM

Psalm 1:6

3. *ungodly (wicked)*

Romans 5:10

4. *enemy of God*

Ephesians 2:2

5. *child of disobedience*

Ephesians 2:3

6. *child of wrath [Note: "Of wrath" refers to what people are recipients of, not what they do.]*

REDEEMABLE IN CHRIST

Matthew 5:13

7. *salt of the earth*

Matthew 5:14

8. *light of the world*

John 1:12

9. *son (child) of God*

John 15:15

10. *friend of Jesus*

Romans 8:17

11. *heir of God and joint heir with Christ*

Romans 8:37

12. *more than a conqueror*

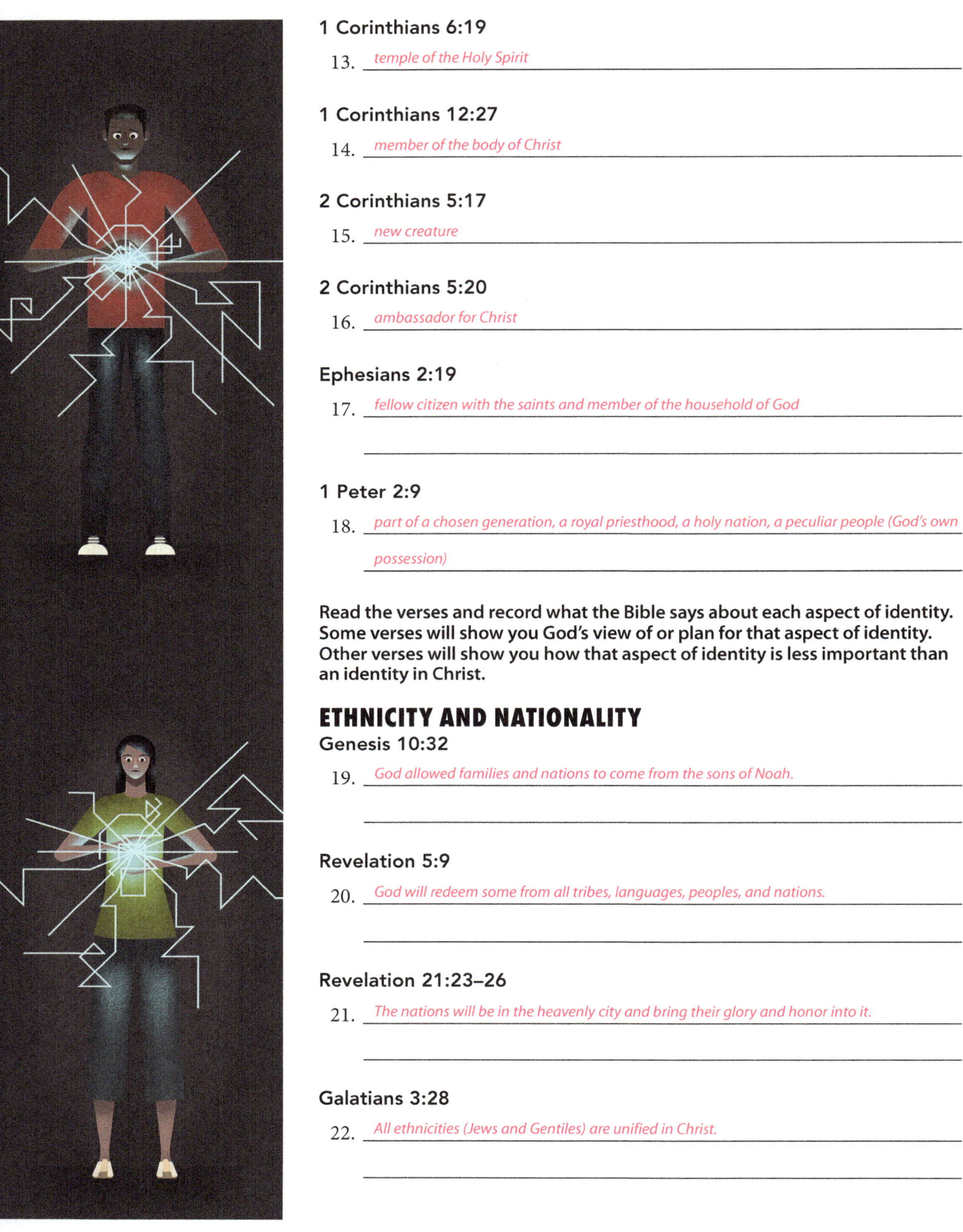

1 Corinthians 6:19

13. *temple of the Holy Spirit*

1 Corinthians 12:27

14. *member of the body of Christ*

2 Corinthians 5:17

15. *new creature*

2 Corinthians 5:20

16. *ambassador for Christ*

Ephesians 2:19

17. *fellow citizen with the saints and member of the household of God*

1 Peter 2:9

18. *part of a chosen generation, a royal priesthood, a holy nation, a peculiar people (God's own possession)*

Read the verses and record what the Bible says about each aspect of identity. Some verses will show you God's view of or plan for that aspect of identity. Other verses will show you how that aspect of identity is less important than an identity in Christ.

ETHNICITY AND NATIONALITY

Genesis 10:32

19. *God allowed families and nations to come from the sons of Noah.*

Revelation 5:9

20. *God will redeem some from all tribes, languages, peoples, and nations.*

Revelation 21:23–26

21. *The nations will be in the heavenly city and bring their glory and honor into it.*

Galatians 3:28

22. *All ethnicities (Jews and Gentiles) are unified in Christ.*

GENDER, MARRIAGE, AND SINGLENESS

Genesis 1:27

23. *God made humans male and female.*

Proverbs 18:22

24. *Finding a wife (getting married) is a good thing.*

1 Corinthians 7:32, 34

25. *Singleness gives people more time to care about the things of the Lord and serve Him well.*

Matthew 22:30

26. *There will be no marriage after the resurrection, so being a husband or wife is not more important than one's identity in Christ.*

STRENGTH AND WISDOM

Proverbs 20:29

27. *The glory of young men is their strength. [Note: You may also point out that a "grey head" refers to an older person's wisdom, which comes from life experience.]*

Proverbs 4:7

28. *Wisdom is the most important thing you could strive to get.*

1 Corinthians 1:27, 29–30

29. *God uses things that seem foolish and weak to the world to confound (defeat) the mighty and the wise so that He will get the glory. Christ is our wisdom.*

WORK

Genesis 1:28

30. *God blessed mankind with the Creation Mandate, which included work.*

Genesis 2:15

31. *God gave Adam a specific job to work on (before the Fall).*

Luke 10:38–42

32.

BELONGINGS

Ecclesiastes 5:19

33. *Wealth and possessions are gifts from God to enjoy.*

Luke 12:15

34. *Our lives are not made up of our possessions.*

Hebrews 11:24–26

35. *Moses valued the reproach of Christ above the treasures in Egypt.*

Write a prayer of thanksgiving to God for who you are. Incorporate the foundation for your identity, as well as aspects of your identity that make you unique.

Answers will vary but should include their value as an image-bearer, their value in Christ if

they are Christians, and various aspects of their unique identity.

CASE STUDY: HUMAN AND ANIMAL VALUE

In 2019 the states of New York and Virginia made it legal for a pregnant mother to abort her unborn child as late as the ninth month of pregnancy. The lawmakers said the purpose was to increase women's control over their bodies. They wanted women to be able to choose whether to keep their babies. New York lawmakers claimed that they were simply updating the laws already in place, although pro-life groups disagreed.

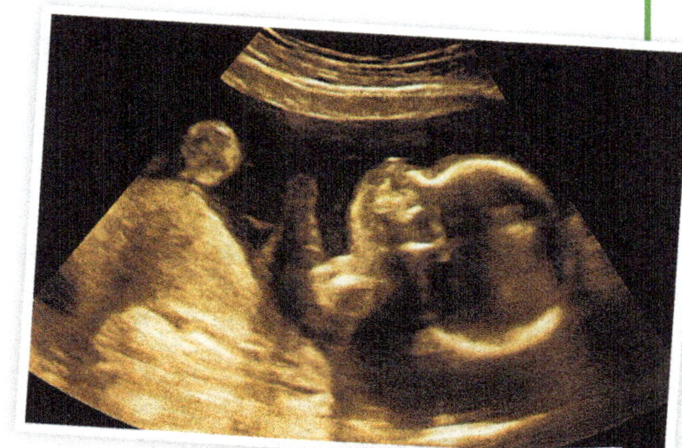

About the same time, other people were concerned about the lives of baby sea turtles hatching on beaches. Conservationists in certain areas discouraged locals and tourists from using outside lights at night at their beach houses. Why? Because the newly hatched sea turtles were getting distracted from their instincts to walk toward the sea. The outside lights were confusing the orientation of the sea turtles. Many walked toward those lights—and away from the ocean where they would find food and be protected from predators. Thus baby sea turtles were more likely to die because of house lights on the beach.

Use what you have learned already in this course to answer the questions.

1. What do those who supported and passed the abortion laws believe about the value of an unborn baby?

   They did not highly value unborn babies but valued the desires of the mother who could

   choose to kill her baby.

2. What do those who promoted turning off lights along beaches believe about the value of baby sea turtles?

   Those people valued the lives of the sea turtles and wanted to keep them from being killed.

3. Why should believers who have a biblical worldview be concerned about saving the lives of unborn human babies?

   Unborn babies are people and have the same value because of their creation by God, His

   image in them, and the fact that Christ died to redeem them. God expects believers to love

   their neighbors as themselves.

4. Why should believers who have a biblical worldview and know the Creation Mandate be concerned about saving the lives of baby sea turtles?

God has given humans dominion over the earth to rule it well. It is not good dominion to create a situation that hurts baby sea turtles' ability to get to the ocean and possibly causes them to die. To rule well under God's rule is to care for His creation and not purposelessly kill it.

5. Why do human babies have more worth than baby sea turtles?

Humans are made in the image of God. Sea turtles are not.

6. What should change in the situations described in the case study, based on a biblical view of human value?

There should not be laws that allow people to kill babies before they are born.

Basics for a Biblical Worldview

By now, you know quite a few things about your fallen nature from God's description of it in Scripture. It's not always easy to be honest about yourself and this fallen nature. Recognizing your fallen nature shows you your need for redemption and can help you focus on certain areas that require growth.

Below are descriptions of different levels of fallenness. Some areas of your life may evidence more fallen direction and other areas more of Christ's redemptive work. These levels will be different for everyone. You probably struggle more in certain areas than in others. Be honest with yourself and with God as you complete the self-assessment.

Mark the sentence that best describes you.

1. How are you participating in your relationship with God?

   ○ I am mostly consistent with daily Bible reading and prayer.

   ○ I want to do these daily, but I am not consistent at all.

   ○ I don't read my Bible daily or pray daily, and I don't really want to.

2. How is your relationship with your parents?

   ○ Although we disagree sometimes, I mostly obey and honor my parents.

   ○ I struggle to show respect to my parents and obey them.

   ○ I don't respect or obey my parents.

3. How is your relationship with your siblings?

   ○ Although we disagree sometimes, I mostly get along with my siblings.

   ○ I struggle to be kind to my siblings and avoid arguments.

   ○ I don't want to be with my siblings at all.

4. How are your relationships with authorities?

   ○ I respect and obey authority almost all the time.

   ○ I struggle to respect and obey authorities.

   ○ I don't respect or obey authorities.

5. How are your relationships with friends?

   ○ Although I could be a better friend, I have many friends that I get along well with.

   ○ I have friends, but we don't always get along.

   ○ I don't have friends, or I don't get along with the ones I have.

6. How do you use your free time?

- ○ I use most of my free time in a variety of God-honoring activities.
- ○ I struggle with doing things I shouldn't in my free time.
- ○ I do things my parents wouldn't approve of during my free time.

7. How do you use technology (gaming, communication)?

- ○ I try not to let technology take my time with others or the time I need for other responsibilities.
- ○ I struggle with technology taking more of my time than it should.
- ○ I spend so much of my time focusing on technology that I don't interact well with others around me.

8. How do you use language?

- ○ I usually use appropriate language and am honest with what I say.
- ○ I struggle with bad language or with lying.
- ○ I use bad language and lie.

9. How do you use your money?

- ○ I usually use my money appropriately.
- ○ I struggle with saving money for more important things.
- ○ I use my money on things that don't last.

10. What is your attitude toward conflict?

- ○ I try to have peace with others.
- ○ I struggle to stay out of fights.
- ○ I thrive on conflict and like to start fights.

11. What is your attitude toward possessions?

- ○ I am usually careful about things I choose to pursue, and I work at being content with what I have.
- ○ I struggle with wanting the latest gear or gadget.
- ○ I have to have the newest thing!

You evaluated the fallenness in yourself in a number of areas. Now, we're looking at the good news. God works in believers to restore His image in them. The Bible often talks about sanctification with the words *holy* and *holiness*, since the point of sanctification is for you to be holy, as God is holy. Sanctification happens immediately when you trust Christ as your Savior—God sees you as holy and set apart for Himself in Christ. Sanctification also happens throughout your life, as you take on the resemblance of God's family in your values, beliefs, and actions. God is active in this process, and believers should be active as well.

Read the verses and record the actions of God and believers in accomplishing sanctification. At the end, summarize how the actions restore the believer to the image of God. If you are a Christian, you may choose to summarize how God is sanctifying you and how you are supposed to take part in the sanctification process.

GOD'S PART

John 17:15–17

1. *Jesus asked the Father to sanctify His disciples through the truth—God's Word.*

Romans 6:22

2. *God sets believers free from sin and makes them His servants (slaves) in order to be holy.*

Romans 8:29

3. *God has already determined that believers will be conformed to the image of His Son.*

2 Corinthians 5:17

4. *God makes those in Christ new creatures (creations).*

Ephesians 2:10

5. *God created believers to walk in good works.*

THE BELIEVER'S PART

Matthew 5:48

6. _Believers should be perfect (mature) like their Father._

Romans 12:1–2

7. _Believers are to present their bodies as a living sacrifice to God. They should renew their minds so that they will be transformed and be able to discern what is the will of God._

Ephesians 2:10

8. _Believers are to walk in the good works that God created for them to do._

Ephesians 4:20–24

9. _Believers should put off the old man, be renewed in their minds, and put on the new man, which is created to be righteous and holy like God._

Colossians 3:9–10

10. _Believers should not lie since they have put off the old man. They have also put on the new man that is renewed in knowledge after the image of the Creator. [Note: Answering that the believer should actively put off the old man and put on the new man is not without merit here also, since the Greek possibly supports that.]_

1 Peter 1:15–16

11. _Believers should be holy in all their conduct because God is holy._

SUMMARY

God sanctifies believers by His Word, frees them from sin, and conforms them to the image of His Son. God makes them new creatures to do good works in Christ. The goal for believers is to be like their Father. They are to renew their minds to be transformed. They are to put off the sinful old man and put on the new man in order to be holy and like their Creator. [Note: Students may also make these concepts personal to themselves.]

Basics for a Biblical Worldview

THE FLESH

You learned in Section 4.6 that the flesh is always present within everyone—including believers. Believers have a constant battle within themselves between their new nature in Christ and their flesh.

Read the verses and answer the questions. At the end, summarize a biblical description of the flesh.

Romans 7:18–19

1. How did Paul know that nothing good dwelt in his flesh?

   He could not do the good things he wanted to do. He did evil instead.

2. What truth do you learn about mature Christians by hearing Paul admit his struggle with the flesh?

   Even mature Christians struggle with the flesh; the flesh won't go away at some point in your Christian life.

3. How does Paul's wording about what was in him relate to Section 4.6?

   He said that his flesh was in him working against him, just as Section 4.6 talks about the enemy within.

Romans 8:13

4. What is the danger of the flesh?

   It brings death.

5. What is the remedy for this danger?

   The believer, with the help of the Spirit, has to kill the flesh's desire to do bad things.

6. How serious is the struggle with the flesh?

   It is a life-and-death struggle.

Romans 13:14

7. What are believers *not* supposed to do for the flesh?

   plan, think of, or provide for a way to fulfill its desires

8. Based on this verse, what do you think the flesh will do if the believer doesn't obey the command?

The flesh will take advantage of the way the believer thinks in order to fulfill its desires.

9. How might thinking of your flesh as your enemy help you obey this command?

I wouldn't want to supply what my enemy needs or give it help.

10. What should believers do to help themselves think and act rightly?

They should put on the Lord Jesus Christ.

Galatians 5:16–17

11. How are believers able to resist the flesh?

by walking in the Spirit

12. What is the battle within the hearts of those who have the Spirit?

a battle between the flesh and the Spirit

13. How does this battle affect believers?

They cannot do what they truly want to do.

SUMMARY

The flesh inside people is not good and causes believers to be unable to do the good things they want to do. The flesh with its desires brings death and must be killed itself. The flesh will take whatever opportunities to fulfill itself that believers give it. The flesh is in conflict with the Spirit. The flesh is the enemy of believers.

Basics for a Biblical Worldview

INNER OPPOSITION STRATEGIES

Read the verses and record the strategy each one gives for fighting the flesh.

Luke 9:23

1. *Deny yourself and take up your cross daily.*

John 8:31–32

2. *Know the truth from what Jesus has said (and, by extension, from the Bible) in order to be free from sin.*

Romans 6:6, 9, 11–13

3. *Recognize that you are dead to sin in Christ and alive to God. Yield to God instead of sin.*

Romans 8:31

4. *Recognize that God is greater than the flesh and He is on your side.*

Romans 12:21

5. *Do good to overcome evil.*

Romans 13:14

6. *Put on the Lord Jesus Christ and do not plan, think of, or provide for ways to fulfill your flesh's desires.*

1 Corinthians 10:12–13

7. *Don't be so proud that you forget to be careful not to fall. Look for the way of escape from temptation and take it.*

2 Corinthians 6:14, 16

8. *Don't have strong relationships with unbelievers that cause you to have to work together (since it's impossible to have real harmony).*

Galatians 5:16

9. *Walk in the Spirit.*

Galatians 6:7–8

10. *Remember that you will reap what you sow, either corruption or everlasting life.*

Colossians 3:1–2

11. *Seek and desire heavenly things, not earthly things.*

1 Timothy 1:18–19

12. *Hold on to your faith and a good conscience so that you can fight well.*

2 Timothy 2:22

13. *Flee the evil desires of young people and run toward righteousness, faith, love, and peace with mature believers.*

Hebrews 4:15–16

14. *Go boldly to the throne of grace to get God's grace to help you resist temptation.*

Hebrews 12:1–2

15. *Lay aside the weights and sins that keep you from running the race well, and look to Jesus as the example of how to patiently persevere and finish well.*

Use ideas from the verses to develop a personal strategy for battling your flesh.

Possible answers: I will pray when temptation comes. I will look for ways to do good instead of evil. I will turn off the TV. I will get rid of the books that make me think sinfully. I will stop hanging out with the friends that tempt me to have a bad attitude.

Basics for a Biblical Worldview

The fallen world appeals to the fallen nature in each of us. You have looked at Making Connections charts before to evaluate categories for their creational structure, fallen direction, and redemptive direction. Here you will look at the fallen direction in various appeals of the world, determine the creational structure they are bending, and decide how to best counteract them with biblical worldview thinking.

Read the verses and complete the chart to evaluate the world's appeals to you through your eye gate.

Approval	The world advertises products to boost your self-image and others' view of how "cool" you are.
Creational Structure	Genesis 1:27–28; Proverbs 16:18 Every person is a creation of God and is under His authority. He is to receive all glory.
Fallen Direction	*This appeals to my sinful pride. This makes me most important in life instead of God.*
Redemptive Direction	I should seek approval from God. My view of myself and others' views of me are less important than what God thinks of me.
Family	The world offers movies and TV shows that present parents as the enemy of children.
Creational Structure	Exodus 20:12 *God expects children to honor their parents.*
Fallen Direction	This appeals to the rebellion in my heart as a child, which looks for reasons to disobey or disrespect my parents.
Redemptive Direction	I should recognize the sinful presentation of family roles and reject that way of thinking before it affects my own behavior.
Attention	The world offers popular clothing styles that are immodest.
Creational Structure	1 Corinthians 6:19–20; 1 Thessalonians 4:4–6 God has given people bodies to honor and glorify Him. Believers are the temple of the Holy Spirit. They are set apart to be holy.
Fallen Direction	This appeals to my desires to draw attention to myself and to take the focus off God as the one who should receive the glory from my body.
Redemptive Direction	*I should make clothing choices that do not draw attention to and glorify myself but glorify God.*

Read the verses and complete the chart to evaluate the world's appeals to you through your ear gate.

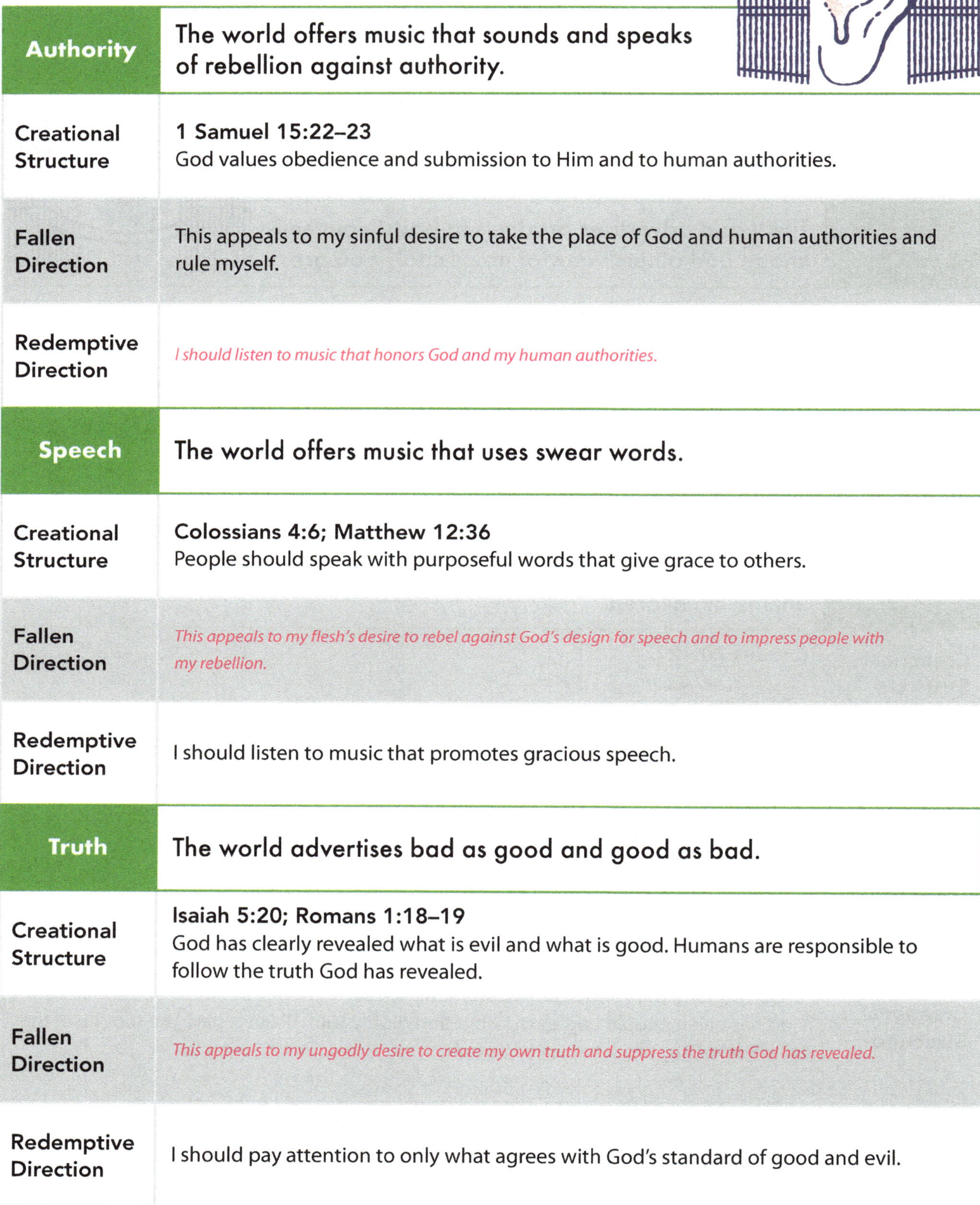

Authority	The world offers music that sounds and speaks of rebellion against authority.
Creational Structure	**1 Samuel 15:22–23** God values obedience and submission to Him and to human authorities.
Fallen Direction	This appeals to my sinful desire to take the place of God and human authorities and rule myself.
Redemptive Direction	*I should listen to music that honors God and my human authorities.*
Speech	The world offers music that uses swear words.
Creational Structure	**Colossians 4:6; Matthew 12:36** People should speak with purposeful words that give grace to others.
Fallen Direction	*This appeals to my flesh's desire to rebel against God's design for speech and to impress people with my rebellion.*
Redemptive Direction	I should listen to music that promotes gracious speech.
Truth	The world advertises bad as good and good as bad.
Creational Structure	**Isaiah 5:20; Romans 1:18–19** God has clearly revealed what is evil and what is good. Humans are responsible to follow the truth God has revealed.
Fallen Direction	*This appeals to my ungodly desire to create my own truth and suppress the truth God has revealed.*
Redemptive Direction	I should pay attention to only what agrees with God's standard of good and evil.

Basics for a Biblical Worldview

Read the verses and complete the chart to evaluate the world's appeals to you through your pride.

Competition	The world says that second place is the first loser.
Creational Structure	Ecclesiastes 9:10; Philippians 2:3 God wants people to do their best but more importantly to put others before themselves.
Fallen Direction	*This appeals to my desires to win and look down on the "losers" and to not care about having a right attitude when I do not win.*
Redemptive Direction	I should do my best in all I do and have a Christlike attitude about whatever place I finish.

Possessions	The world advertises products that imply you deserve the best.
Creational Structure	Psalm 103:2–5, 10; James 4:10 God wants people to have a humble attitude in light of their position before Him.
Fallen Direction	This appeals to my selfishness and ignores how God provides for my needs in ways that the world thinks are less than the best.
Redemptive Direction	*I should be thankful with what God provides for me and recognize that I do not deserve His gifts.*

Work	The world advertises a life that is fun and easy with no responsibilities.
Creational Structure	Genesis 2:15–17; Proverbs 20:4 God made mankind to work and to follow His standards.
Fallen Direction	*This appeals to my self-centered desire to live with my own purposes and standards. This appeals to my laziness.*
Redemptive Direction	I should fulfill the responsibilities that God gives me and accept them as His good gifts to me.

OUTER OPPOSITION STRATEGIES

Jerry Bridges uses the illustration of an airplane to explain how a believer grows in sanctification. Just as an airplane needs both wings, so a believer needs both dependence on God and self-discipline to say no to temptation and yes to holy living. He says that throughout the Bible the writers make it clear: "'Man's part is to trust and work. God's part is to enable the man or woman to do the work.' . . . God's work does not make our effort unnecessary, but rather makes it effective." As you battle outside opposition, you will need to work hard using many strategies. But you will also need strategies for depending on God, and the best way to depend on God is through prayer.

Match the reference with its strategy or strategies. Then match each strategy with the category it is part of.

Reference
1. Psalm 119:9
2. Psalm 119:11
3. Psalm 119:105
4. Psalm 119:115
5. Psalm 119:133
6. Nehemiah 4:8–9
7. Matthew 26:41
8. Romans 12:1
9. Romans 12:2

#	Strategy	Category
6	I can pray for God's protection from enemies of His work.	A
3	I can use the Word of God as a light to guide me.	B
9	I can renew my mind in order to be transformed.	B
1	I can obey the Word of God.	B
6	I can engage in guarding against enemies of God's work.	B
5	I can ask God to guide my actions with His Word so that no iniquity would rule me.	A
8	I can present my body as a sacrifice to God.	B
2	I can memorize the Word of God.	B
7	I can pray to be kept from temptation.	A
9	I can refuse to let the world make me like itself.	B
4	I can keep evildoers away from me in order to keep the commandments of God.	B
7	I can watch to escape temptation.	B

A. Depending on God

B. Doing my part

10. Philippians 1:9

11. Philippians 1:10

12. Philippians 1:11

13. Colossians 1:9

14. Colossians 1:10

15. Colossians 1:11

16. 1 Timothy 4:12

17. 1 Timothy 4:13

18. 2 Peter 1:5–7

_17_	I can pay close attention to Bible reading, preaching, and teaching.	_B_	
_10_	I can pray for my love to grow in knowledge and discernment.	_A_	
_13_	I can pray that I will be filled with knowing God's will in wisdom and spiritual understanding.	_A_	
_16_	I can refuse to let others convince me I'm too young to live right.	_B_	
_14_	I can pray that I will walk worthy of the Lord.	_A_	
_18_	I can diligently add to my faith virtue, knowledge, self-control, patience, godliness, brotherly kindness, and love.	_B_	
_12_	I can pray that I will be filled with the fruits of righteousness by Jesus Christ.	_A_	
_14_	I can pray that I will be fruitful in every good work.	_A_	
_16_	I can be an example to others in my speech, my lifestyle, my love, my faith, and my purity.	_B_	
_11_	I can pray that I will approve excellent things.	_A_	
_15_	I can pray that God will strengthen me to be patient and joyful.	_A_	

A. Depending on God

B. Doing my part

Basics for a Biblical Worldview

Culture developed in obedience to the Creation Mandate. It meets the basic needs humans have when trying to fill and subdue the earth. Modern cultures came through many changes over time. But all cultures developed from those basic needs. Many factors influence how cultural products develop. Think about the varieties of local materials, geography, weather, society structures, and cultural ideas about beauty. Each culture is unique because of the unique set of factors of its place and people. That set of factors affected the way the local people developed each cultural product.

You will research a cultural category to explain how humans have worked to meet a need within their culture and, as a result, created products. You should include how the factors around the culture affected the early development of the products. Then you will connect the development with modern culture. Last, you should determine how the development obeys God's Creation Mandate.

Read through the following analysis as an example.

CULTURAL CATEGORY

transportation of cargo

NEED MET

People needed to move goods from one place to another as they made goods in many distant locations.

CULTURAL PRODUCT THAT DEVELOPED TO MEET THE NEED

One main factor affecting cargo transportation in America has been the size of the country. (American states are similar in size to European countries.) Although Americans are spread out geographically, they work together as one large society. In order for Americans to get goods to other Americans, they had to develop road and rail systems. They also made vehicles to move as many goods as possible over long distances.

The Conestoga wagon is an example of early vehicle development. Obviously it had limitations. Trains were eventually built and improved. They could transport much larger loads of goods faster over long distances. Tractor-trailers also began to carry loads over the extensive road system. The interstates have been especially helpful for this development. Later, airplanes were included as a way to transport cargo.

CREATION MANDATE'S COMMANDS OBEYED

With transporting goods anywhere by vehicles, Americans can fill the earth. They can get the goods they need to subdue and have dominion. Receiving food and other items essential to life helps them be fruitful and multiply as a people. To make transportation possible, Americans also subdue those parts of creation that make it difficult to move large loads across large spaces.

Trace a cultural category from its original need through the factors that shaped a particular cultural product. Then explain how the cultural product obeys one of the Creation Mandate's commands.

CULTURAL CATEGORY

Possible answers: communication, technology, education, travel, food preparation

NEED MET

Answers should recognize the basic need met by the cultural category, such as relationships,

productivity, improving skills, or physical needs.

CULTURAL PRODUCT THAT DEVELOPED TO MEET THE NEED

Answers should demonstrate thoughtful analysis of the development of a cultural product

within the chosen cultural category to meet a certain need, including local factors that

influenced the development and related systems or processes that helped the product be

used.

CREATION MANDATE'S COMMAND OBEYED

Answers should develop one of the commands specifically: being fruitful and multiplying,

filling the earth, subduing, or having dominion over the earth.

Basics for a Biblical Worldview

Weeding out the fallen direction in parts of your culture is just the beginning of your task. You'll need to think hard about how to create things that will push your culture toward God's true, good, and beautiful design for culture. Analyze the description of creational structure and fallen direction in the cultural categories. The Bible gives guidance about how cultures should follow God's purposes for these categories. The Bible also shows how cultures bend God's purposes. Use your biblical worldview to write ways you can push your modern culture in a redemptive direction. You can use culture to honor God and love your neighbor.

Complete the chart. *Answers will vary.*

Music	
Creational Structure	Music was part of prepared temple worship as well as spontaneous celebrations of God's work in the lives of His people. Both professional and amateur musicians were involved in worshiping God. Music is also shown as ministering to troubled hearts to soothe them.
Fallen Direction	Music may be done in an attempt to rebel against God. Music may try to replace the fear of the Lord with godless amusement. Some people may twist God's intentions for music by limiting it to professional musicians or to worship at particular times or places.
Redemptive Direction	*I can sing, play, listen to, and write music to worship the Lord, to celebrate His work in our lives, and to minister to hearts. I can use my skills in music purposefully for the benefit of others. This is music that is redemptive and shows love for my neighbors.*

Art	
Creational Structure	In the tabernacle and temple, art included images of things from nature (like palm trees and oxen), symbols of spiritual realities not seen (like the cherubim), and even images not based on reality but imagination (like blue pomegranates). All of these kinds of art were used for worshiping God.
Fallen Direction	Art is fallen when it is used for idolatry. The images that ancient cultures created were for the worship of idols. Many pieces of art are still being created for false gods. Art is also bent when it is crafted to bring selfish pleasure to people or specifically to rebel against God and the truths of the Bible.
Redemptive Direction	*I can create art in a variety of styles, but it should reflect the truth, goodness, and beauty of God, spiritual realities, or the designs God put into His creation. With this kind of art, I enhance the lives of my neighbors.*

Literature

Creational Structure	We have clear evidence of the structure of literature because God revealed Himself in the greatest of books, the Bible. He used a large variety of genres to do this. He also set the standard for true, good, and beautiful communication, even when having to describe sinful people and events.
Fallen Direction	Fallen literature communicates the lies of the world and the Devil instead of communicating God's truth. Any genre bent in a fallen direction may glorify sin or lead a reader to idolize someone or something above God.
Redemptive Direction	*I can read books that help teach me God's truth and how it applies to my life and the world around me. By recommending books like this to my neighbors, I can love them with the truth of God.*

Movies

Creational Structure	God mainly used stories to reveal Himself in His Word. True, good, and beautiful stories reflect God's storytelling. Scripture uses both images and music in storytelling. For example, the Psalms are hymns for worship, and God had prophets use object lessons to tell the story of His message.
Fallen Direction	Similarly to fallen literature, fallen movies may portray sinful actions in an untruthful way or in a way that tempts viewers to act sinfully too. Movies can promote idolatry, tell lies, and glorify ugliness and sin. They can appeal to the viewers' sinful desires of the flesh and eyes and their pride.
Redemptive Direction	*I can watch movies that help me be more like Christ. Movies with redemptive direction can help me understand the hurts of others and love them better. I can promote movies that will help my neighbors understand God's truth.*

Social Media

Creational Structure	Since God is a Trinity, communication is part of His nature. He made men and women to relate to Him and to each other. Being created in God's image makes communication both natural and necessary for people. God gave people the ability to create tools to communicate with each other and grow relationships.
Fallen Direction	Human communication is also fallen. Social media can be used in twisted ways: lying, slandering, spreading rumors, bullying, and other sinful practices. It can be used for communicating pictures or videos that are unkind or crude.
Redemptive Direction	*Using social media to help maintain good friendships is loving my neighbor. Encouraging a friend or rebuking the sin of a friend are good uses of communication. Sharing the gospel of Christ is loving my neighbors by introducing them to the Savior.*

Basics for a Biblical Worldview

DEFINING BIBLICAL WISDOM

Complete the concept definition map about biblical wisdom. Use the verses in each box. *Answers will vary.*

EXAMPLES
WHAT ARE SOME ILLUSTRATIONS?

Proverbs 10:31

The righteous speak wisdom.

Proverbs 11:12

Those who lack wisdom despise their neighbors; those who have wisdom know when to be quiet.

Proverbs 15:21

Those who lack wisdom enjoy foolishness; those who have wisdom walk in the right way.

1 Corinthians 1:23–24

Those who are called recognize Christ as the wisdom of God.

CHARACTERISTICS
WHAT IS IT LIKE?

Proverbs 9:10

It begins with the fear of the Lord; it is related to the knowledge of the Holy One.

Proverbs 11:2

It is related to humility (lowliness).

Proverbs 14:8

It helps people understand their way.

Ecclesiastes 2:13

It is better than folly.

1 Corinthians 1:30

It comes from God in the person of Christ Jesus.

James 3:17

It is pure, peaceable, gentle, full of mercy and good fruits, impartial, and sincere.

BIBLICAL WISDOM

COMPARISON TERMS

Proverbs 21:30

understanding, counsel

DEFINITION
WHAT IS IT?

a spiritual understanding for life choices that comes out of my relationship to God

WISDOM AND SCHOOL

Wisdom is crucial for a young person to mature well. Biblical wisdom teaches you the truth about reality and your relationships with God and others. It blesses you with many things important for maturing, and it protects you from the dangers of living outside the truth. It helps you act rightly.

There is someone you must know in order to know the wisdom from God. This knowledge is the first step in learning biblical wisdom.

Read the verses and answer the question.

1 Corinthians 1:23–24; Colossians 2:1–3

1. God's wisdom is in whom?

    Christ

Read the verses and record the positive benefits of wisdom that help a young person mature well. Then record the negative consequences of fool-ishness that a young person avoids by being wise instead.

Proverbs 4:3–19
(Wisdom is personified as a woman in these verses.)

2. Positive benefits gained

    Wisdom preserves and keeps those who love it (verse 6). It will exalt and honor those who promote and embrace it (verse 8). It will be like a decoration of grace and a beautiful crown to you (verse 9). It will give you many years of life (verse 10). It is life to you (verse 13).

3. Negative consequences avoided

    It will keep you from being hindered and from stumbling (verse 12). It will keep you from the path of the wicked (verse 14). It will keep you from doing wickedness toward others (verse 16). It will keep you from violence (verse 17). It will keep you from spiritual darkness (verse 19).

You've learned by now that God wants you to love your neighbors enough to do good works to benefit them. Biblical wisdom gives you the tools to do just that. And so does the wisdom you learn through your schoolwork.

Unit 5 has also taught you that good works can be accomplished through many fields of work. You will brainstorm how school can help someone do good works in a particular field of work. You may choose a field you are interested in, one your parents are involved in, or one you know a lot about.

Choose a field. Explain how school helps build the wisdom necessary to love one's neighbors through that field.

4. Field of work

    Possible answers: scientist, law enforcement, lawyer, doctor, pastor, business manager

5. Wisdom through school

    Answers will vary but should demonstrate thoughtful analysis of the kinds of things school would teach that would give wisdom for the doing the job well. For example: Learning the communication skills necessary—reading, writing, and speaking. Learning the history of the field and its established principles—natural laws, civil laws, theology, economic principles. Learning the math required—chemical formulas, forensic mathematics, budgeting, statistics.

6. Opportunities to love neighbors as a result of this wisdom

    Answers will vary but should demonstrate examples of good works done for others. For example: Scientists develop new products for things like health, communication, travel, and productivity. Law enforcement learns the laws to keep people safe and to minimize crimes. Lawyers use the law to make things just for people. Doctors help people be healthy and heal when they are injured or sick. Pastors help people to learn about spiritual life in Christ and to grow in that life. Business managers provide products and services that people need for living in the society.

Basics for a Biblical Worldview

BIBLICAL ATTITUDES TOWARD CULTURAL PRODUCTS

Every cultural category of products has a good creational structure within it. The Fall, however, corrupted everything—including the cultural products that humans make. As you might expect, products can be redeemed too. You need to discern what is the appropriate attitude to have toward each product. Many Christians review cultural products from a biblical worldview to help others, like you, choose what attitude to have.

The following verse and questions will help us judge what is worthy of condemning, critiquing, consuming, or copying.

Finally, brethren, whatsoever things are true, whatsoever things are honest, whatsoever things are just, whatsoever things are pure, whatsoever things are lovely, whatsoever things are of good report; if there be any virtue, and if there be any praise, think on these things. (Philippians 4:8)

True: Is it true to life? Do natural consequences occur for behavior? Does it reflect the natural and spiritual structure God built into creation?

Honest: Is it worthy of respect?

Just: Are the bad punished and the good rewarded? Do things come back to a just balance?

Pure: Does it avoid showing things that are impure or evil?

Lovely: Does it follow principles of beauty like proportion, harmony, simplicity, and complexity? Does it attract? Does it illustrate well the order of God's creation?

Of good report: Does it have beautiful speech? Is it recognized as valuable? Does it have a good reputation?

In addition to thinking about the positive standards from Philippians 4:8, you must also consider objectionable content. Objectionable content includes bad language, immodesty, violence, and the use of tobacco, alcohol, or illegal drugs. Just as in the Bible, objectionable elements in a story are not necessarily bad if they are being presented as sinful or harmful and warn you from participating. You can evaluate the objectionable content to make sure it does not fall into these three categories.

Unnecessary: Is it without purpose in the story?
Graphic: Does it give more details of bad things than is absolutely necessary for the story?
Bad moral tone: Does it attempt to manipulate right and wrong? Does it imply that good is evil and evil is good?

Below is a chart you can use to rate cultural products. If the final total is a negative number, the product should most likely be condemned. The closer the total is to zero, the more you may need to critique the product with careful discernment. The higher the total, the more you may feel comfortable to consume and copy the product. Your score on a product may differ from someone else's because your evaluation may be more or less critical of certain aspects.

	POSITIVE (YES) SCORE: +1	NEUTRAL (NOT SURE) SCORE: 0	NEGATIVE (NO) SCORE: –1
True			
Honest			
Just			
Pure			
Lovely			
Of good report			

	POSITIVE (NO) SCORE: +1	NEUTRAL (NOT SURE) SCORE: 0	NEGATIVE (YES) SCORE: –1
Unnecessary			
Graphic			
Bad moral tone			
TOTALS		+ 0	– =

Read the excerpts and information from the movie and book reviews. On a separate sheet of paper, label each movie and book as "condemn," "critique," or "consume and copy." You may use the chart to score each product, but be sure to explain why you chose your response.

1. THE AVENGERS (MOVIE)

As expected, the action violence is frequent in THE AVENGERS, with nonstop action in the final half hour. However, unlike the violent tone in the new Batman movies, there's always a sense of light and good.

Characters have to humble and sacrifice themselves (including risk their lives).

In addition to the information from the reviewer, this movie includes some immodesty, a crude joke, intense violent action (although without blood), and some bad language scattered throughout.

2. THRONE OF GLASS (BOOK)

There was a surprising amount of gruesomely described dead bodies.

There were visits from the spirit world and demonic creatures.

Celaena Sardothien [the main character] is an *assassin*.

The reviewer also mentions that the author tries to make sense of the main character's actions by referencing her past as an orphan. The reviewer does not agree, though, that the main character should be excused for having pleasure in killing. Also, the characters often use bad language.

3. STAR WARS: A NEW HOPE (MOVIE)

STAR WARS [A New Hope] is great science fiction . . . [and] the end has good triumphing over evil. . . . To move the plot along, the idea of the Force . . . works; as a theological statement it is a New Age travesty. . . . Practice caution because of the mysticism that forms its world view.

In addition to the information from the reviewer, there are a few uses of bad language and intense violent action and gory details.

4. SPIDER-MAN: INTO THE SPIDER-VERSE (MOVIE)

SPIDER-MAN: INTO THE SPIDER-VERSE is a terrific, enjoyable animated adventure with clever, funny writing. The story's energy seldom stalls. The movie has lots of cartoon action violence and some light slapstick violence. Some of the action violence is intense, so caution is advised for children. Otherwise, the movie is family-friendly. SPIDER-MAN: INTO THE SPIDER-VERSE has an uplifting Christian, moral worldview. Its redemptive pro-family themes extol love, sacrifice, forgiveness, doing the right thing, saving others, and getting a second chance.

In addition to the information from the reviewer, there are crude references and some bad language.

5. EASY A (MOVIE)

EASY A is a cleverly written film with some appealing characters and performances, some funny moments, and even some heart-warming moments. However, there's too much offensive content. In fact, some of it is rather abhorrent. For example, there are more than 50 PG-13 obscenities and profanities and strong lewd content, including innuendos about adult activity with teenagers. EASY A also has some drug references, implied nudity and underage drinking. Even worse, the movie contains politically correct, clichéd, self-righteous mockery of Christians, including Christian clergy. There's absolutely no excuse for such abhorrent content.

6. AVATAR (MOVIE)

AVATAR is a visually stunning, but shallow and abhorrent, adventure pitting evil human capitalists against heroic, spiritually in-tune alien creatures on the planet Pandora. Its story, dialogue, and characters are weak and shallow. Also, its New Age, pagan worldview contains extremely anti-capitalist content with a strong Marxist overtone. It promotes group-think and argues in favor of the destruction of the human race.

In addition to the information from the reviewer, there are instances of graphic immodesty, crude jokes, graphic violence, and bad language throughout.

7. JOHNNY TREMAIN (BOOK)

It's about humility and kindness, loyalty and bravery.

It's set during a war. . . . There's fighting.

Rab and Johnny intentionally get Dove drunk to get information out of him.

Although the story ends on a sad note, you're still left with a feeling of strong patriotism.

The reviewer also mentions that the theme of friendship is strong. Also, there are a few inappropriate words.

8. A CINDERELLA STORY (MOVIE)

Wonderfully written, . . . the movie starts off at a high level of good
humor and moral fundamentals. . . . The movie extols kindness,
love, compassion, decency, and all the cardinal Christian virtues in a
positive, winsome, attractive way. . . . A CINDERELLA STORY is a
must-see movie for all ages.

In addition to the information from the reviewer, there are some instances
of immodesty, crude talk, and bad language.

9. LORD OF THE RINGS: THE RETURN OF THE KING (MOVIE)

RETURN OF THE KING is one of the great movie masterpieces
that weaves many biblical principles and allegorical Christian met-
aphors into a magnificent story, but it is too scary and intense for
younger children.

Much of the fear comes from suspense, not actually showing blood
and gore, although there is some.

In addition to the information from the reviewer, the movie contains
some immodesty, intense frightening scenes, and one occurrence of bad
language.

10. THE PERFECT MAN (MOVIE)

THE PERFECT MAN is a light comedy with moral lessons on priori-
tizing family and recognizing self-worth and one's gifts instead of one's
dating status. . . . Romance takes second place to values such as family,
self-worth and facing one's problems without running away.

In addition to the information from the reviewer, the movie contains
flirting, a confession of unfaithfulness in a relationship, and one obviously
immoral character.

11. CITY OF BONES (BOOK)

There is quite a bit of violence and some scary elements.

The Lord's name is taken in vain . . . at least 10 times, along with
other profanities.

Madame Dorothea is rumored to be a witch.

God doesn't appear to have any role at all.

I can't discount the evil. I can't shake off the uncomfortable feeling
that the book gives me.

This story had so many other dark elements and references. If it had
just been about killing demons, . . . this might've been more accept-
able. But it runs so much deeper than that here.

God made men and gave them a specific role. But since the Fall, many unbiblical ideas have developed about what men are or should be. Some husbands do not love their wives as the partners in life that God designed them to be. Some men let women rule over them, even though God created men to selflessly lead the family and church in serving Him.

The Bible shows that God created men and women to be the best team for obeying His Creation Mandate. A husband is to be the leader in that team and treat his wife as God's gift to him. While some men are gifted for singleness, God planned for most men to be married.

In this Making Connections chart, you will evaluate quotations and commercials for the fallen direction in the role of men. You will also determine the creational structure they are bending and decide how the fallen direction can be counteracted with redemptive direction.

Read the verses, which show how men should relate to women, and complete the chart.

Authority	"Love is what . . . makes the civilized man permit a woman to drag him around by the nose." —Helen Rowland
Creational Structure	**Genesis 2:18** God gave the man a wife as a helper in the work God gave him to do.
Fallen Direction	Men who fail to take leadership in their homes have twisted God's plan.
Redemptive Direction	**1 Corinthians 11:3** *Husbands are the authority over their wives and should take that responsibility seriously.*
Love	"Before marriage, a man declares that he would lay down his life to serve you; after marriage, he won't even lay down his newspaper to talk to you." —Helen Rowland
Creational Structure	**Genesis 2:23** God made the woman from a part of the man to show how close their relationship ought to be.
Fallen Direction	*Husbands who do not treat their wives with the love they would give themselves have twisted God's plan.*
Redemptive Direction	**Ephesians 5:25, 28** Husbands are to love their wives as Christ loved the church. They should always treat their wives as they would treat themselves.

Leadership	"At first, every man seems to fancy that it takes nothing but brute force and determination to run an automobile or a wife." —Helen Rowland
Creational Structure	**Genesis 1:27–28** *God made husbands and wives to work together as partners to accomplish the Creation Mandate.*
Fallen Direction	Husbands who do not honor their wives or try to understand them as those they are supposed to lead are not following God's plan for accomplishing the Creation Mandate.
Redemptive Direction	**1 Peter 3:7** Husbands should treat their wives with honor as the weaker partner. They should seek to understand their wives as they live and work together.
Work	A commercial shows a man making a mess and a frustrated woman having to clean up after him.
Creational Structure	**Genesis 2:15, 18** God made the man as the one originally responsible for the work. Men are capable workers and should work with their wives.
Fallen Direction	Commercials that show men as dumb and women as the only capable ones are denying God's plan for men and women to be partners and for men to be the ones accountable.
Redemptive Direction	**1 Timothy 3:1, 4–5, 12** *God expects overseers (pastors) and deacons to rule their own households well, which means men are capable of doing it and should work at it.*
Dominion	A commercial shows a husband as too dumb to figure out something on a computer, so his wife does it for him.
Creational Structure	**Genesis 1:26** God gave mankind His image and the ability to take dominion over all the earth.
Fallen Direction	*Commercials that show men as dumb are denying the way God made men and the purpose He gave them.*
Redemptive Direction	**1 Corinthians 16:13** Men should act on whatever God has given them to do, knowing that God has equipped them for obeying His commands.

Basics for a Biblical Worldview

God made women and gave them a specific role. He created Eve to be a helper suitable for Adam. This role does not make women less important than men—it makes them partners in obeying the Creation Mandate. As you have learned, God gave the man the ultimate responsibility of leading the family and the church. In those areas, the woman is a partner to him and not an authority over him. God has created men and women to complement each other with the strengths and weaknesses of their different roles.

Today, our fallen society wants women and men to be the same. It wants women to act like men in areas that are typically men's strengths. But God designed for women's strengths to be in areas of life that are typically men's weaknesses. To make women like men lessens the woman's best way of influencing society.

In this Making Connections chart, you will evaluate quotations for the fallen direction in the role of women. You will also determine the creational structure they are bending and decide how the fallen direction can be counteracted with redemptive direction.

Read the verses, which show how women should relate to men, and complete the chart.

Work	"I suppose I could have stayed home and baked cookies and had teas, but what I decided to do was to fulfill my profession." —Hillary Clinton
Creational Structure	**Genesis 1:27–28** God designed women to be a part of the team with men to fill the earth and have dominion over it.
Fallen Direction	Women who mock other women who work for their families in the home are not recognizing this valuable work as part of God's Creation Mandate.
Redemptive Direction	**Titus 2:3–5** *Wives should not neglect caring for their husbands and children. Helping to manage the family and home is God's honorable calling to the wife and mother.*
Submission	"I don't think a female running a house is . . . a broken family. It's perceived as one because of the notion that a head is a man." —Toni Morrison
Creational Structure	**Genesis 2:15, 18** *The dominion work was given directly to Adam. Eve was given to Adam as an appropriate helper. The final responsibility was Adam's since he was the head of the family.*

Fallen Direction	Denying the order of authority God created when He created the first family twists God's design. People promote single-parent households as being just as good as God's plan.
Redemptive Direction	**1 Corinthians 11:3; 1 Timothy 2:12–13** Godly women will submit to the authority God has given to men in the family and the church.
Physical Abilities	"My coach said I ran like a girl. I said if he could run a little faster he could too." —Mia Hamm
Creational Structure	General revelation demonstrates that God created men's bodies stronger than women's.
Fallen Direction	*The world tries to make men's and women's physical abilities the same (or even says women's are greater than men's), but in reality they are not.*
Redemptive Direction	**1 Peter 3:7** Women should not be offended that men were designed to be stronger and protective. Wives should accept the honor their husbands give them as the weaker vessel.
Family	"A woman needs a man like a fish needs a bicycle." —Irina Dunn
Creational Structure	**Genesis 2:24** God said that the man and woman were to become one as a new family.
Fallen Direction	Saying that women do not need men goes against the biblical design of men and women marrying to build families together.
Redemptive Direction	**Genesis 1:28** *Women should not refuse to get married (unless God has gifted them for singleness) or speak badly of marriage since God intended for husbands and wives to multiply and fill the earth.*

Basics for a Biblical Worldview

COMMUNITY, FRIENDSHIP, AND JESUS

Read the verses and answer the questions.

Genesis 1:28

1. How did God's blessing-command for Adam and Eve to fill the earth reveal His plan for community?

   As they filled the earth, numerous communities would be created.

Proverbs 17:17

2. How are friends helpful to us as part of our community?

   They love us at all times.

Proverbs 27:6, 9–10, 17

3. How would a friend wound in a way that demonstrates faithfulness?

   A friend will tell you truths that may hurt but that you need to hear.

4. How can a friend bring joy to another?

   by giving good counsel

5. In God's plan for community, how might friends be more valuable than relatives?

   God planned for us to have a community of friends nearby, who could help us when relatives live far away.

6. How does a friend make another better?

   by grinding away at the dullness to make the other person sharp (more effective or skillful)

John 3:26–30

7. According to the example in verse 29, how can friends in a community follow the commandment to love their neighbor?

   Friends can show love to others in the community by rejoicing in their times of celebration.

8. How was John the Baptist a true friend to Jesus?

   He rejoiced in Jesus' gain and was not jealous.

James 4:4

9. How can we break our friendship with God?

   by being a friend of the world

Proverbs 17:9

10. How can we ruin our friendships with others?

    by reminding friends of their mistakes

Mark 5:15–19

11. What did Jesus expect the man whom He had freed from demon possession to do for his friends?

    to tell his friends what Jesus had done for him and how Jesus had shown mercy to him

12. If you are saved, what does Jesus expect you to do for your friends?

    to tell them what Jesus has done for me

John 15:12–15

13. What is the greatest way a friend can show love for another?

    by laying down his life for the other

14. How did Jesus prove that He was a friend to the disciples? (15:13, 15)

    He lay down his life for them. He told them things that a master would not tell his servants.

    He communicated with them as friends.

Basics for a Biblical Worldview

Some people and cultures see the community as more important than the individual. The individual is expected to yield his rights for the good of the community. Other people and cultures see the individual as more important than the community. The individual expects to exercise his rights even at the expense of the community. As you saw in Section 7.1, neither extreme fits well with a biblical worldview.

The Bible gives plenty of information about the creational structure—and the fallen direction—of both individuals and communities. Both are important and necessary, yet both can be twisted by sin. As you interact with the verses below, try to determine how they indicate a balance between individuals and different kinds of communities.

Read the verses and complete the chart with the biblical information about communities and individuals. The verses may imply truths about only one category, so you will need to think carefully how to make application for the other category.

	Kinds of Communities	Individuals
Genesis 1:27; 2:18	God created both man and woman because He knew that it was not good for man to be alone. Every person should be part of a family.	God made each individual in His image, both men and women. Each individual is precious as an image-bearer of God.
Genesis 9:6	*With the increase of people in the world, government formed for ensuring justice according to God's plan.*	*One who murders an image-bearer forfeits his own life, because an individual's life is valuable in God's sight.*
Psalm 86:9; Acts 17:26–27	*God made all the nations that have ever existed with the purpose of their bringing glory to His name. God planned where and when these communities of people would dwell.*	*Nations worship God only when individuals in that nation seek God and worship Him.*
Deuteronomy 4:7–10	*God made Israel a nation. In order for the Israelites to remain faithful to God as a community, God required them to teach their children His truths.*	*Each individual Israelite had a personal responsibility to remember God and obey Him and to train up his or her children correctly to do the same within the community.*

	Kinds of Communities	**Individuals**
Ecclesiastes 4:8–12	*A community of friends is helpful for the individual because it gives him a reward for his labor in sharing, someone to pick him up when he falls, someone to help meet his needs, and someone to help fight against attacks.*	*Individuals who live in community reap great benefits from helping each other and can live with greater purpose than serving oneself.*
Matthew 12:36–37	*No community will stand with the individual when he gives account for careless words (neither to help nor to be accused).*	*Each person must individually give account for his careless words.*
John 9:13–16, 30–34	*The Pharisees, the religious community, rejected Jesus as the Messiah and tried to influence the formerly blind man, the individual, to conform to their views.*	*The formerly blind man had to stand against the community of the religious leaders to defend Jesus as being sent from God.*
Acts 12:5–10	*The church, the community of believers, prayed for the individual Peter who was in prison.*	*Peter, as an individual in need, benefited from the community of his church by their prayers.*
Romans 10:8–9	*The community can preach the gospel but cannot decide for the individual to confess Jesus as the resurrected Lord.*	*The individual must confess that Jesus is the resurrected Lord in order to be personally saved.*
1 Corinthians 11:27–33	*The Lord's Supper is taken in the community of the church.*	*The individual is to examine himself at the Lord's Supper to confess any sin before partaking. The individual who does not do this may be punished by God.*
Hebrews 10:24–25	*The community of the church should assemble regularly to encourage each other to continue in good works.*	*The individual is responsible to assemble with the church, to provoke others to love and good works, and to encourage others.*

DEFINING THE CHURCH

Complete the concept definition map about the church. Use the verses in each box. *Answers will vary.*

EXAMPLES
WHAT ARE SOME ILLUSTRATIONS?

2 Corinthians 6:16

It is illustrated as the temple of God.

Ephesians 5:25–27

It is illustrated as the wife in a marriage relationship with Christ.

1 Peter 2:5, 9

It is illustrated as a spiritual house, a chosen generation, a priesthood, a holy nation, and a peculiar people.

1 Peter 5:1–4

It is illustrated as a flock of sheep under the elders (pastors) and under the chief Shepherd.

CHARACTERISTICS
WHAT IS IT LIKE?

Matthew 16:18

Jesus builds it and keeps the gates of hell from prevailing against it.

Acts 2:41

It is baptized believers formed into a group.

Acts 2:42

They gather to learn doctrine, have fellowship, share in the Lord's Supper, and pray.

Acts 2:44–45

They share what they have with those in need.

1 Corinthians 12:13

It is unified into one body by the Holy Spirit's baptism of each individual.

Ephesians 4:15–16

It is joined together by the Head, Jesus Christ, and grows in Him.

CHURCH

COMPARISON TERM

Acts 19:32–41

assembly

[Note: Explain to students that the same Greek word is used for both secular, public gatherings and for "church."]

DEFINITION
WHAT IS IT?

The church is a group of baptized believers who assemble to learn doctrine, have fellowship, share the Lord's Supper, and pray. They are unified by the Holy Spirit with Jesus Christ as the Head and builder of their group.

WORD PICTURES OF THE CHURCH

Christ's church is too marvelous to illustrate in only one way, and no single word picture captures all of its glory in Him. Below are several verses that represent the church in various ways. Think through what new truths God is communicating by giving us these mental images based on things we already know.

Read the verses and answer the questions.

1 Timothy 3:15

1. What are the word pictures used to represent the church?

   the house (household) of God; the pillar and ground of the truth

2. What are some truths they teach?

   The church is the family of God. God has made the church to be what supports and displays

   His truth.

3. What then are some privileges the church has?

   Possible answers: They have rights as children of God, and they have the ability to grow

   into Christ's likeness. They are entrusted with God's truth.

Ephesians 2:21–22

4. What is the word picture used to represent the church?

   a holy temple

5. What are some truths it teaches?

   The church is joined with Christ and is growing as a dwelling place for the Lord. The Spirit

   has a role in building the church.

6. What then are some privileges the church has?

   Possible answers: They themselves are the dwelling place for the Lord. No longer are they

   separated from the presence of God, as in the time of the tabernacle and temple.

Colossians 1:18; Ephesians 4:4, 11–12, 15–16

7. What is the word picture used to represent the church?

the body of Christ

8. What are some truths it teaches?

Christ is the Head of the body; He is most important. The body is to be built up (edified) by all the members. Every member in the body must contribute to its growth in love.

9. What then are some privileges the church has?

Possible answers: They will be raised from the dead as Christ was. They have the same unity and hope in the calling of God. They have fellow members to build up and to be built up by.

Ephesians 5:22–32

10. What is the word picture used to represent the church?

the bride of Christ (the relationship of a wife to her husband)

11. What are some truths it teaches?

The church should submit to Christ. Christ loved the church and gave Himself for it. He is purifying the church for His return. As a husband and wife are one flesh, Christ is one with the church.

12. What then are some privileges the church has?

Possible answers: They are loved by Christ. They have been saved by the gift of Christ's life. They are made one with Christ. They have the care and provision of Christ.

Basics for a Biblical Worldview

WHICH CHURCH?

You learned in Section 7.3 that every believer should become a member of a local church. What should a believer look for in a church? This: A group of people committed to fulfilling the responsibilities—the mission—that they have been given in Scripture. See what the Bible says about these responsibilities and then analyze how a modern church is still fulfilling these responsibilities today.

Read each passage and match it with the corresponding responsibility of the local church. Some references will be used more than once. Then relate the responsibility to how a modern local church might be fulfilling it. *Answers will vary for the modern church fulfillment.*

A. Matthew 18:15–17	F. 1 Corinthians 11:23–28	J. 1 Timothy 1:3–4
B. Matthew 28:18–20	G. Galatians 6:1	K. 1 Timothy 2:1–2
C. Acts 1:8	H. Philippians 2:1–2	L. 1 Timothy 4:13
D. Acts 2:42	I. Colossians 3:16	M. 1 Timothy 5:1–2
E. Acts 8:4–5		

	Verses	Fulfillment by Members in a Modern Church
Doctrine	B, D, J, L	*teaching all of what Christ commanded; preaching, teaching, and listening to sound doctrine in services, Sunday school, small-group studies, and Bible institute classes; reading the Bible*
Fellowship	D, H	*spending time loving each other and having unity in Sunday school classes, group activities, and small-group studies*
The Lord's Supper	D, F	*participating in communion on a regular basis; examining themselves before participating*
Prayer	D, K	*praying in services, Sunday school, and small groups; having prayer lists so that the members are aware of needs to pray for*
Evangelism	B, C, E	*sending missionaries to other nations to make disciples; witnessing to unbelievers in personal relationships and community outreaches; preaching; having kids' clubs or vacation Bible school*
Discipleship	B, I, M	*helping others to become more like Christ through small-group Bible studies, Sunday school, counseling, one-on-one accountability, and mentoring*
Church Discipline	A, G	*removing an unrepentant member from church membership; restoring a member who repents*

Interview a church member about how he or she practices the above responsibilities in a local church. Write a summary. *Answers will vary.*

COMMUNITY ORGANIZATIONS

Community organizations meet the needs of individuals in society in ways that a government, other individuals, or even a family cannot. They provide necessary services to the people of the community—making their lives better in multiple areas. As you learned in Section 7.4, community organizations include volunteer fire departments, senior citizen centers, homeless shelters, food distribution centers, and many more.

You will practice discerning not only the ways community organizations serve their neighbors but also whether they are operating from a biblical worldview. You yourself may be able to bring salt and light into a community organization. For example, one place that provides a great way to meet and serve people is the local recreation department. Sports leagues give opportunities to both kids and adults to develop socially and physically. And they often provide the opportunity Christians are looking for to meet their neighbors' spiritual needs.

Research the mission statements of three organizations in your local community. Find organizations from different areas of life such as health, finances, recreation, physical needs, or spiritual needs.

Answer the questions with information from your research.

ORGANIZATION 1

1. What is the organization's name and mission statement?

   Example organization: Miracle Hill; "Miracle Hill exists that homeless children and adults receive food and shelter with compassion, hear the Good News of Jesus Christ, and move toward healthy relationships and stability."

2. How does the organization meet the needs of the community?

   It provides housing and food to meet the physical needs of homeless people. It also provides a gospel witness to try to bring the unsaved to Christ for a new life in Him.

3. How could this mission statement be adjusted to reflect a biblical worldview?

   This one already has a Christian perspective but might specifically include Christ as the center of healthy relationships and stability.

ORGANIZATION 2

4. What is the organization's name and mission statement?

____

____

____

5. How does the organization meet the needs of the community?

____

____

____

6. How could this mission statement be adjusted to reflect a biblical worldview?

____

____

____

ORGANIZATION 3

7. What is the organization's name and mission statement?

____

____

____

8. How does the organization meet the needs of the community?

____

____

____

9. How could this mission statement be adjusted to reflect a biblical worldview?

____

____

____

You learned in Section 7.6 that government is part of God's good design for the world. While it is structural (a necessary result of obeying the Creation Mandate), government involves fallen people, who inevitably push it in a fallen direction. Believers should help push government back in a redemptive direction: to rule properly under God's rule. They can use both political involvement and their witness of Christ. Christ must reconcile individuals to God so that they can rule properly under Him.

Read the verses and complete the chart.

Romans 13:1–7	
Creational Structure	*Government is ordained (instituted) by God. The power of government is from God. It is to be a terror to evil works. It is to praise those who do good. It deserves the tribute and customs (taxes and revenue) it charges for its services.*
1 Peter 2:13–14	
Creational Structure	*Government is to be submitted to for the Lord's sake. It is to punish evildoers and to praise those who do well.*
Deuteronomy 1:12–18	
Creational Structure	*Government is to judge cases between citizens. It is to judge righteously. It is to hear cases from both the small and the great. The judgment of government ultimately belongs to God.*
Fallen Direction	*When government shows partiality, favoring the great and despising the poor or fearing someone of great wealth or importance, it is pushing in a fallen direction.*
Redemptive Direction	*Government can be pushed back toward its structure by upholding fairness for all and not making wrong judgments because of fear.*

Psalm 82:1–5
Fallen Direction — *When government judges unjustly and approves of wicked people, it is pushing in a fallen direction.*
Redemptive Direction — *Government is pushing in a redemptive direction when it defends the poor and the orphans, does justice to the afflicted, delivers the poor, and rescues people from the wicked.*

Proverbs 29:4
Fallen Direction — *When government takes bribes, it is pushing in a fallen direction.*
Redemptive Direction — *Government that works with good judgment is pushing back against corruption.*

Jeremiah 22:2–3
Fallen Direction — *When government does violence to outsiders, orphans, or widows, or sheds innocent blood, it is pushing in a fallen direction.*
Redemptive Direction — *Government should deliver victims from their oppressors and protect the innocent from harm.*

Basics for a Biblical Worldview

BIBLICAL PURPOSES OF GOVERNMENT

Why do people need government? What did God make government for? God gave an example of what good government looks like when He established Israel as a nation governed by His authority. We are able to read about the reasons why He created this government so that we can apply the principles to government today. You will examine these Scriptures to determine God's purposes for government.

Read the verses and explain each biblical purpose or purposes given for government.

1 Kings 10:9

1. Purpose of government

   to do judgment (righteousness) and justice

2. How does this action promote order?

   As the king does justice, the order of law will be established.

Psalm 72:1–7, 11–14

3. Purposes of government

   to judge with righteousness, deliver the needy, and break the oppressor

4. How does this action promote justice?

   As the king judges in righteousness, justice is maintained for both those who do right and those who do wrong.

5. How does this action deal with poverty?

   The king punishes those who oppress the poor and delivers the needy from violence.

Genesis 9:6; Numbers 35:30

6. Purpose of government

   to execute murderers by a just process

7. How does this action promote justice?

Romans 13:3–4

8. Purpose of government

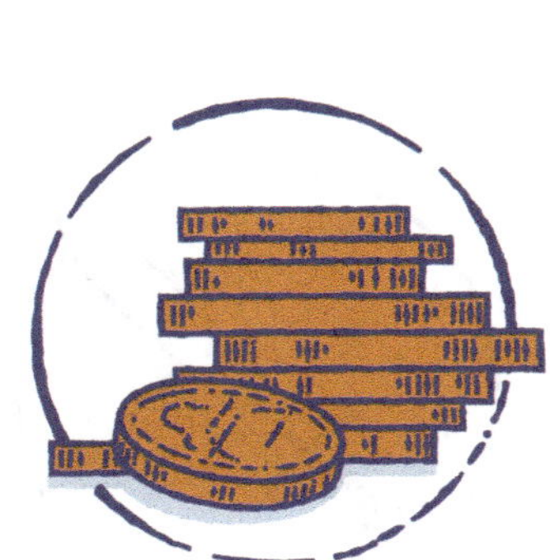

9. How does this action promote justice?

10. How does this action promote safety?

11. How does this action promote order?

Leviticus 19:35–36

12. Purpose of government

13. How does this action promote justice?

Leviticus 19:9–10

14. Purpose of government

15. How does this action deal with poverty?

Deuteronomy 24:10–13

16. Purpose of government

    to ensure people treat the poor fairly in business dealings

17. How does this action deal with poverty?

    It protects the poor from losing their basic physical possessions.

18. How does this action promote justice?

    It ensures that the rich do not use their power to treat the poor badly.

Exodus 22:2–3
(Apply the principle for the individual to the government.)

19. Purpose of government

    to provide for a defense against attackers

20. How does this action provide for national defense and promote safety?

    It provides for nations to defend themselves when intruders would do harm.

21. How does this action promote order?

    It discourages nations from attacking and breaking up the order established between nations.

FALSE WORLDVIEWS AND IDOLATRY

Worldviews that are not based on the Bible have basic characteristics that make them idolatrous. They fall into two categories. In Romans 1:18–23, Paul describes a worldview that has completely turned away from God's truth to worship other things. Romans 10:1–4 describes a worldview that is theistic (believing in God) yet still idolatrous. You will analyze these passages for some idolatrous characteristics of false worldviews.

Read the verses and answer the questions. At the end of each group, summarize two things: their worldview and characteristics of idolatry that they portray.

UNBELIEVING GENTILES

Romans 1:18

1. What are two general descriptions of the condition of those Gentiles who hold a worldview of unbelief?

   ungodliness and unrighteousness

2. What do they do with God's truth?

   They suppress (hold) it by their unrighteousness.

Romans 1:19–20

3. How did they get the truth?

   God has manifested it in them. The invisible things about God, His power and divinity, are seen in the creation.

4. What is the result of their having the truth?

   They are without excuse.

Romans 1:21

5. How did they treat God, whom they knew?

   They did not give Him the glory He deserved as God.

6. What was their attitude about what they had been given?

   They were not thankful.

7. What happened to their thinking?

   It became vain.

8. What happened to their hearts?

   They were darkened.

Romans 1:22

9. What did they claim to be?

wise

10. What were they really?

fools

Romans 1:23

11. What did they do with God's glory?

They exchanged it for lesser things like men and birds and animals and creeping things.

SUMMARY

They believed they could live without God and His standard of truth and righteousness

as part of their big story. They believed they could ignore the truth about God in creation.

As a result of their beliefs, they suppressed the truth of God, acted in unrighteous ways,

and gave God's glory to something else that was created by God.

SUMMARY

Possible answers: (1) Deliberately lives in unrighteousness against God's truth (Romans

1:18); (2) denies God's power (Romans 1:20); (3) denies that God is God (Romans 1:20);

(4) worships other things besides God (Romans 1:23).

Basics for a Biblical Worldview

UNSAVED ISRAEL

Romans 10:1

12. What did Paul desire for Israel?

that they would be saved

Romans 10:2

13. What was wrong with Israel's zeal for God?

It was not based on knowledge.

Romans 10:3

14. What did Israel not understand, or was ignorant of?

the righteousness of God

15. What did their lack of understanding give them boldness to attempt?

to seek to be righteous in themselves

16. How were they responding to the righteousness of God (which includes God's righteous way to save sinners)?

They were not submitting to it.

Romans 10:4

17. Why is Christ the end of the law?

He fulfilled the law perfectly.

18. How does Christ's life demonstrate the impossibility of sinners establishing their own righteousness?

Sinners are unable to live as perfectly as Christ lived.

SUMMARY

They did not see themselves as sinners who needed God's righteousness in Christ. They

ignored God's redemption in their big story of the world. As a result of their beliefs, they

sought to establish righteousness for themselves through their works.

SUMMARY

Possible answers: (1) Denies or ignores God's righteousness (Romans 10:3); (2) seeks to

establish personal righteousness without God (Romans 10:3); (3) does not submit to

the righteousness of God through Christ (Romans 10:3–4).

Basics for a Biblical Worldview

Few things have influenced current cultures more than social media. And few, if any, social media platforms have had a greater impact than Facebook®. With over two billion users, Facebook's community is more populous than any country. Facebook changed how people interact, share, make friends, and develop online identities. It has inspired many other platforms like Instagram®, Snapchat®, and TikTok®.

Mark Zuckerberg is the man behind Facebook. He believes that the next level of community to develop is the global community. His goal is for Facebook to play a major part in that. He believes that the more freedom people have to communicate, the better the world will become. He also believes that the community can come together to develop standards about objectionable content. He says cultures can develop their own standards:

> The guiding principles are that the Community Standards should reflect the cultural norms of our community, that each person should see as little objectionable content as possible, and each person should be able to share what they want.

Zuckerberg's words point to a belief that all people are basically good. The problems in the world come from limiting community and free speech.

Zuckerberg has seen Facebook bring people together who would never have connected before. But it has enabled predators to take advantage of the innocent. It has also made bullying easier than ever. Facebook has brought customized ads to a new level. But it has also divided countries with ads that ignore other viewpoints. It has enabled politicians to engage with thousands of people. But it has also allowed false information to be spread. Refugees of war have been connected with those who can meet their needs. But terrorist groups can also recruit new soldiers to their causes. Facebook has opened up an entirely new culture of connection. As a result, it has been a force for both good and bad around the world.

Answer the questions.

1. What are some of Mark Zuckerberg's basic beliefs, which reveal his worldview?

   He believes that we need to develop the global community. He believes in free speech for everyone. He believes people can have their own standards for objectionable material. He believes that people are basically good and that problems come from limiting free speech.

2. How has Zuckerberg's worldview affected the way he has developed Facebook?

He has created a way for the whole world to connect through the internet. He has created a way for people to freely express themselves in a public way. He has allowed all kinds of material to be published on Facebook. He has given freedom because he believes people are basically good.

3. Why has Facebook had such a widespread effect on modern cultures?

Facebook has allowed people to come together from across all kinds of communities. Zuckerberg's belief in free speech has allowed more people to make their voices widely heard than ever before.

4. How has Facebook been good for modern cultures?

It has brought people together who could not have otherwise connected. It has allowed people to voice their views and opinions who would not normally have had a public way to do that. It lessens cultural misunderstandings or conflicts because people understand other cultures better.

5. How has Facebook been bad for modern cultures?

It has allowed criminals access to those they would hurt. It has allowed cyberbullying. It has allowed false information to be presented as truth. It has allowed hateful groups to recruit people. It has given these groups a bigger voice to affect their cultures and find others to support them.

Basics for a Biblical Worldview

ISLAM VERSUS CHRISTIANITY

You've been presented with an introduction to the worldview of Islam. In this activity, you will contrast the worldviews of Islam and Christianity. You may use Section 8.2 as well as additional research.

Complete the charts with answers to the five worldview questions.

Christianity	*The Triune God created everything out of nothing. He spoke the world into existence. I am a creation made in the image of God.*
Islam	*Allah created everything out of nothing. I am the superior creation of Allah, designed to be a master of creation while submitted to his mastery.*

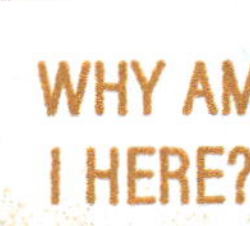

Christianity	*I am here to enjoy a relationship with God through Christ and to glorify God with my life by fulfilling the Creation Mandate.*
Islam	*I am here to submit to Allah, to find, fear, and respect him, and to rule over his other creations.*

Christianity	*All people fell in Adam. Adam's disobedience to God passed on a sin nature to every person born, so we all are sinners. As the head of the covenant, Adam also brought a curse on the earth when he sinned. Sin and the effects of the curse are what's wrong with the world.*
Islam	*Allah brings suffering to test people to see their obedience and submission to him. He also punishes with suffering those who rebel against him. His created natural laws have consequences when broken. There is suffering for these purposes, but the world is not broken, nor are people innately sinful.*

Christianity	*Because all are sinners, we have no ability to restore our relationship to God. In Christ, God made the way to justly punish sin and reconcile sinners to Himself. Those who repent of their sin and trust Jesus, the Savior, will be restored in their relationship to God. One day Christ will restore all creation back to God.*
Islam	*I am made right by my submission and obedience to Allah. Allah will have mercy as I try to do right by his rules and seek his mercy when I fail. Ultimately, Allah decides who will spend eternity in paradise and the decision about eternal salvation belongs only to him. He makes that decision based on the faith people have in him and their obedience to his message through the prophet Muhammad.*

Christianity	*My relationship to God determines my destination. If I have repented of my sin and trusted Christ, I am restored to God and will one day live with Him in perfect fellowship on the new earth. If I have rejected Christ as Savior, I will spend eternity separated from God in the lake of fire, a place of torment.*
Islam	*I seek to obey Allah and to gain his mercy in order to go to paradise. I may spend time in punishment after I die in order finish paying for my sins so that I can enter paradise. If I fully reject Allah and the Islamic faith, I will go to hell when I die.*

Use the characteristics of idolatry to show how Islam is idolatrous.

1. Denies or ignores God's righteousness (Romans 10:3)
2. Seeks to establish personal righteousness without God (Romans 10:3)
3. Does not submit to the righteousness of God through Christ (Romans 10:3–4)

Islam is idolatrous because it denies God's righteous character in contrast with mankind's sinfulness. Its followers seek to establish their own righteousness. Muslims actually worship their own ability to be righteous. They do not submit to the righteousness of God found only in Christ.

Basics for a Biblical Worldview

BUDDHISM VERSUS CHRISTIANITY

You've been presented with an introduction to the worldview of Buddhism. In this activity, you will contrast the worldviews of Buddhism and Christianity. You may use Section 8.3 as well as additional research.

Complete the charts with answers to the five worldview questions.

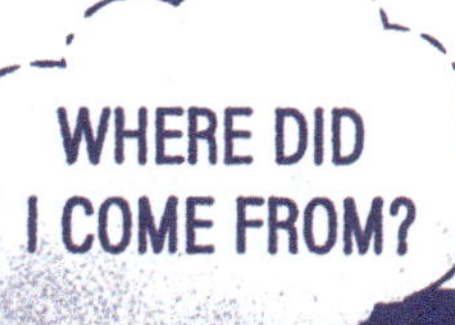

Christianity	*The Triune God created everything out of nothing. He spoke the world into existence. I am a creation made in the image of God.*
Buddhism	*I am really just my perceptions and desires; I have no permanent self. I have been continually reborn into different existences based on my good or bad karma.*

Christianity	*I am here to enjoy a relationship with God through Christ and to glorify God with my life by fulfilling the Creation Mandate.*
Buddhism	*I am here to end my suffering by relinquishing all my desires and thus becoming enlightened (achieving nirvana).*

Christianity	*All people fell in Adam. Adam's disobedience to God passed on a sin nature to every person born, so we all are sinners. As the head of the covenant, Adam also brought a curse on the earth when he sinned. Sin and the effects of the curse are what's wrong with the world.*
Buddhism	*My desires are the problem. I have not yet been enlightened because I still have desires and expectations, which can never satisfy me or bring me happiness.*

Christianity	Because all are sinners, we have no ability to restore our relationship to God. In Christ, God made the way to justly punish sin and reconcile sinners to Himself. Those who repent of their sin and trust Jesus, the Savior, will be restored in their relationship to God. One day Christ will restore all creation back to God.
Buddhism	Things can be made right as I relinquish my desires and simply do good and be good without seeking my own satisfaction. I can save myself from suffering as I let go of my desires.

Christianity	My relationship to God determines my destination. If I have repented of my sin and trusted Christ, I am restored to God and will one day live with Him in perfect fellowship on the new earth. If I have rejected Christ as Savior, I will spend eternity separated from God in the lake of fire, a place of torment.
Buddhism	There is no "I" that continues after death. Personhood is an illusion. The various forces of what appear to be me, along with my karma from this life, will influence the conditions into which I'm reborn.

Use the characteristics of idolatry to show how Buddhism is idolatrous.

1. Deliberately lives in unrighteousness against God's truth (Romans 1:18)
2. Denies God's power (Romans 1:20)
3. Denies that God is God (Romans 1:20)
4. Worships other things besides God (Romans 1:23)

Buddhism promotes unrighteousness against God's truth by denying God-given desires.

It denies God's power to save by seeking salvation in the individual. It does not recognize

any creator God. It worships the enlightened state of nirvana instead of God.

UNBELIEF AS A RELIGION

The Nones claim unbelief to varying degrees. Some do not believe in God at all. They reject the existence of a supernatural realm and believe only in the existence of matter and energy. These are atheists.

Others believe that a god exists or that a god might exist—but humans cannot really know him. No holy book is completely authoritative. God didn't really reveal himself to us. Those who believe a creator god left us to ourselves are deists. Those who believe that, if there is a god, we cannot know him are agnostics.

Remember that even Nones, who say they have no beliefs, are still worshipers. The characteristics of idolatry presented in Romans 1 are just as true of atheism, deism, and agnosticism today as they were of the false Gentile worldview in Paul's day.

Complete the chart with the ways that both types of unbelief fit the characteristics of idolatry.

Deliberately Lives in Unrighteousness against God's Truth (Romans 1:18)	
Atheism	*The atheist seeks to make his own morality based on how he sees the world around him, outside of any absolutes established by God. He disobeys the Word of God in favor of his own ideas and thoughts.*
Deism and Agnosticism	*The deist and agnostic either deny that God has authority or believe that they cannot know it at all. They do not think that they must obey God's Word because they deny it as revelation from God.*

Denies God's Power (Romans 1:20)	
Atheism	*The atheist denies the truth of God's power displayed in the creation around him. He acts as if there is no God and all that people see and experience is from some natural source instead of supernatural actions. He denies the truth of God as the sustainer of everything.*
Deism and Agnosticism	*The deist and agnostic deny the truth of God's power by denying that God has actually revealed Himself in this world through creation. They deny the power of His sustaining work in creation and what that reveals of Him and His care for us.*

Denies That God Is God
(Romans 1:20)

Atheism	*The atheist denies that there is any god at all and thus sets the true God aside as unreal.*
Deism and Agnosticism	*The deist and agnostic might believe in a god, but set the true God aside as not clearly revealed either in creation or the Bible. Instead, they choose to believe in a god that cannot be known or trusted to work in this world.*

Worships Other Things besides God
(Romans 1:23)

Atheism	*The atheist follows a godless science that excludes conclusions based on a divine designer. He worships whatever he values most and may worship science as the answer to everything.*
Deism and Agnosticism	*The deist and agnostic may look to this world for the satisfaction or fulfillment that would be found in God. They worship whatever they value most.*

Basics for a Biblical Worldview

THE NONES' WORLDVIEW

Nones deny God and His revelation in both creation and the Bible. Their worldview is based on the here and now, not on eternity. Their worldview lacks a "higher power" that they would be accountable to or be able to look to for help. As a result of these different lenses, Nones look at life situations very differently from Christians.

Complete the chart with descriptions of the Nones' worldview in these real-life situations and how it contrasts with the biblical worldview.

<table>
<tr><td colspan="2">Moral Crisis</td></tr>
<tr><td>Nones' Worldview</td><td>Possible answers: I decide what is right and wrong based on how I feel or what does the greatest good for the greatest number of people. What is wrong in one situation might not be wrong in another. People have the right to decide for themselves what is right or wrong.</td></tr>
<tr><td>Biblical Worldview</td><td>God has given clear laws and judgments on what is right and wrong. These are absolute standards and do not change for various cultures or situations, though how God's Word is applied to different situations often requires wisdom.</td></tr>
<tr><td colspan="2">Financial Crisis</td></tr>
<tr><td>Nones' Worldview</td><td>Possible answers: My finances are my responsibility. I may be able to look to others for help or loans, but I stand or fall on my own. It's really all up to me to get out of this financial crisis.</td></tr>
<tr><td>Biblical Worldview</td><td>God has given me my finances to manage carefully. He provides for me and is ultimately in control of my income. He will help me to change if I have done wrong or to provide for me if the situation requires it. I can still look to God for help even if I made financial mistakes.</td></tr>
<tr><td colspan="2">Financial Success</td></tr>
<tr><td>Nones' Worldview</td><td>Possible answers: I have successfully gained the wealth I have. I have my wealth because I was able to make money myself. I am now able to spend my money however I want.</td></tr>
<tr><td>Biblical Worldview</td><td>God has given me financial success. He has entrusted me with wealth. I am thankful to Him. I will enjoy the blessings of God, seek to glorify Him, and help others with His good gifts to me.</td></tr>
</table>

Terminal Illness	
Nones' Worldview	*Possible answers: My life is in the here and now. I will live for the things I value most in my final days because this life is all I have. When I die, everything is over for me. Death will be an end of my life, so if I am in pain, it is better for my life to end.*
Biblical Worldview	*I can look forward to being with God for eternity. I should spend my final days as I should spend all my days, living for the Lord and enjoying His gifts of family, friends, and creation. I can trust that my life is in God's hands and will end when He thinks is best.*
Death of Family Members or Friends	
Nones' Worldview	*Possible answers: While I may try to cope by thinking that my family members or friends will live on in my heart, they are actually gone and that is the end of their lives. There is no hope of actually seeing them again.*
Biblical Worldview	*Family members or friends who have died are in heaven or hell. If they were saved, and if I am saved, we will see each other again in heaven and on the new earth where we will live forever.*

Basics for a Biblical Worldview

SOCIETIES' QUESTIONS

The following questions are being asked by societies all over the world. What do you think about these particular social situations? You will learn in Section 8.5 why these questions are being asked.

Answer each question with yes or no and explain your answer. *Answers will vary.*

1. Should an elected official create a law based on the Bible or on the majority opinion of those who elected him?

   Yes, an official who believes the Bible recognizes it as the absolute authority over all of God's creation. No, the official has a responsibility to represent the opinions of those who elected him.

2. Should students be allowed to carry a Bible into a public school?

   Yes, the government should not restrict students' right to read their Bibles while at school. No, students should respect those who do not believe the Bible by leaving their Bibles at home to read there.

3. Should public school officials be allowed to pray publicly before school events?

   Yes, asking divine blessing on a school event should not be considered harmful. No, public school officials should not pray a public prayer, which may conflict with the faiths of some participants.

4. Should a professor at a non-Christian university be allowed to teach creationism as a scientific alternative to the theory of evolution?

   Yes, a Christian professor, or any professor, should be able to teach creation as an alternative to evolution because creationism has scientific validity. No, creationism is based on faith and should not be taught as science in a science classroom.

5. Should a Christian school be allowed to hire only those who agree with their beliefs about doctrine?

   Yes, as a private business, a Christian school should be allowed to include agreement in doctrine as a requirement for hire. No, a Christian school should not discriminate against employees based on religious beliefs.

6. Should a courthouse, or any government building, be allowed to have the Ten Commandments posted on their property?

Yes, any government building should be allowed to post the Ten Commandments because they are foundational to all law systems. No, government buildings should not post the Ten Commandments because they include the Christian belief in the God of the Bible.

7. Should a Christian be allowed to share his faith with others at his government job?

Yes, a Christian should be allowed to share his faith in personal conversations with his coworkers. No, a Christian should not offend others by sharing his faith with coworkers, who have to work with him.

8. Should a public school teacher be allowed to pray with, read her Bible to, and witness to her class?

Yes, a public school teacher should be allowed practice her faith in her classroom with her students. No, a teacher should not use her position of authority over students to make them participate in religious activities that may not be part of their own faiths.

9. Should "In God We Trust" be written on all American currency?

Yes, America was founded on trust in God and His providence, and this truth should be shown on the currency. No, not all Americans agree with this statement, and thus it should not be used to represent everyone.

10. Should national leaders call for national days of prayer?

Yes, national leaders should recognize the power of prayer to change the course of national emergencies or to show trust in God during problems. No, national leaders should not assume that everyone believes in prayer nor force a day of prayer on those who do not.

THE SECULARIST WORLDVIEW

Secularism claims to be neutral and to be the best worldview for a life of peace and success. Do these claims stand up to a biblical worldview?

Examine these claims of secularism from Section 8.5 and answer the questions about its neutrality and effectiveness as a worldview.

"GOD . . . DOESN'T RULE OVER THE 'SECULAR' WORLD."

1. Is this claim neutral? Explain.

   No, it is not neutral because it reveals a religious belief about God.

2. What does Deuteronomy 10:14 indicate is the biblical worldview's understanding of the "secular" world?

   All things belong to God, including things on the earth that are part of daily life. There is no part of the universe that is not under His authority.

"YOU [GOD] CAN OFFER ME . . . SOME INSIGHT FOR MY PERSONAL LIFE, BUT THAT'S AS FAR AS YOU CAN GO."

3. Is this claim neutral? Explain.

   No, it assumes that God rules only one part of a person's life instead of all his life.

4. What does Proverbs 3:5–6 indicate is the biblical worldview's understanding of God's domain?

   Not only should we trust God with all our hearts instead of our own thinking, but we should also acknowledge Him in all our ways.

"ONLY 'NEUTRAL,' 'RATIONAL,' 'NON-RELIGIOUS' VIEWPOINTS SHOULD BE ALLOWED IN PUBLIC."

5. Is this claim neutral? Explain.

   No, it allows what secularists think is non-religious, without acknowledging that their decision is based on their own religious beliefs (what they worship).

6. What does 1 John 2:15 indicate is the biblical worldview's understanding of a person's loves?

"WE SHOULD ALL PUT OUR RELIGION ASIDE WHEN WE COME INTO THE PUBLIC SQUARE."

7. Is this claim neutral? Explain.

8. What does Psalm 119:46 indicate is the biblical worldview's understanding of Christian witness?

"CHRISTIANS [SHOULD] CHECK THEIR FAITH AT THE DOOR TO ALL PUBLIC SPACES."

9. Is this claim neutral? Explain.

10. What does John 15:5 indicate is the biblical worldview's understanding of the Christian life?

MTD BELIEFS

Moralistic Therapeutic Deism holds certain ideas that may sound right and may even appear to come from the Bible but contradict what the Bible actually says. Use what you learned from Section 8.6 to examine these ideas in light of the Bible.

Answer the questions.

WHERE DID I COME FROM?

1. How would MTD answer this worldview question?

   God created me somehow, since he's the one who created the world. [Note: Those who believe in MTD may incorporate evolution into their story of how God created the world and individuals.]

2. How could you give more detail to the MTD belief with Isaiah 44:24?

   God works in the creation of each person; He did not work only in the original creation.

WHY AM I HERE?

3. How would MTD answer this worldview question?

   I am here to be happy and nice.

4. How could you refute the MTD belief with 1 Corinthians 10:31 and the two Great Commandments?

   God says that all we do should bring glory to Him. He is the focus of our lives, not ourselves. We are to love Him with all our being and to love our neighbors as ourselves.

WHAT IS WRONG WITH THE WORLD?

5. How would MTD answer this question?

   People are not good or nice to each other. I am not happy, or I am not as happy as I could be.

6. How could you refute the MTD belief with Jeremiah 17:9 and Romans 8:22?

   The deceitful and wicked hearts of sinners are what is wrong with the world. The whole world groans under the curse of sin as well.

HOW CAN THINGS BE MADE RIGHT?

7. How would MTD answer this question?

   Things are made right when everyone is good and nice to each other.

8. How could you refute the MTD belief with Colossians 1:19–22?

   God made peace through Christ's sacrifice on the cross and will reconcile sinners to Himself

   so that they can be holy before Him.

WHERE AM I HEADED?

9. How would MTD answer this question?

   If I am a nice person, I'll go to heaven when I die. If I'm really evil, I'll go to hell when I die.

10. How could you refute the MTD belief with John 3:16?

    Those who do not believe in Jesus will face eternal death, or separation from God. Those

    who believe in Jesus will have eternal life with God.

Basics for a Biblical Worldview

UNIT 1

Case Study: Fritz Haber's Two-Story View

Dietrich Stoltzenberg quoting Fritz Haber in *Fritz Haber: Chemist, Nobel Laureate, German, Jew* (Philadelphia: Chemical Heritage Foundation, 2004), xxii.

UNIT 3

Discovering Beauty

R. C. Sproul, "Is Beauty in the Eye of the Beholder?," *Recovering the Beauty of the Arts*, lecture 3 (Sanford, FL: Ligonier Ministries, 2003), DVD.

UNIT 4

Making Connections: Identity

Cheyanne Ntangu quoting Pauline Aphiaa in "You Can't Be Black, 'Woke' and Christian," *Artefact Magazine*, January 20, 2017, http://www.artefactmagazine.com/2017/01/20/cant-black-woke-christian/. Bracketed text was written by Cheyanne Ntangu.

Dietrich Stoltzenberg quoting Fritz Haber in *Fritz Haber: Chemist, Nobel Laureate, German, Jew* (Philadelphia: Chemical Heritage Foundation, 2004), xxii.

Rachel Shinnick, "How I Coped with My Career-Ending Injury," Psych Bytes, August 1, 2019, https://www.psychbytes.com/career-ending-injury-affective-cycle-of-injury/.

Journeyman Pictures quoting Ho Jae-woo in "Academic Pressure Pushing S. Korean Students to Suicide," August 10, 2015, https://www.youtube.com/watch?v=TXswlCa7dug&t=20s.

Derek Thompson, "Workism Is Making Americans Miserable," *Atlantic*, February 24, 2019, https://www.theatlantic.com/ideas/archive/2019/02/religion-workism-making-american-miserable/583441/.

Outer Opposition Strategies

Some content taken from page 127 of *The Discipline of Grace* by Jerry Bridges. Copyright © 1994, 2006. Used by permission of NavPress. All rights reserved. Represented by Tyndale House Publishers, a Division of Tyndale House Ministries.

UNIT 5

Making Connections: Culture

Some content drawn from Leland Ryken, "What the Bible Says about the Arts," chap. 2 in *Culture in Christian Perspective: A Door to Understanding and Enjoying the Arts* (Portland, OR: Multnomah, 1986).

Biblical Attitudes toward Cultural Products

MOVIEGUIDE®, review of Marvel's *The Avengers*, https://www.movieguide.org/reviews/star-wars.html.

Harper Collins Alexander, "Throne of Glass—Sarah J. Maas—Book Review," April 4, 2014, https://christianbookreviewsblog.wordpress.com/2014/04/04/throne-of-glass-sarah-j-maas-book-review/.

MOVIEGUIDE, review of *Star Wars*, https://www.movieguide.org/reviews/star-wars.html.

MOVIEGUIDE, review of *Spider-Man: Into the Spider-Verse*, https://www.movieguide.org/reviews/spider-man-into-the-spider-verse.html.

MOVIEGUIDE, review of *Easy A*, https://www.movieguide.org/reviews/easy-a.html.

MOVIEGUIDE, review of *Avatar*, https://www.movieguide.org/reviews/avatar.html.

Harper Collins Alexander, "Johnny Tremain—Esther Forbes—Book Review," October 22, 2013, https://christianbookreviewsblog.wordpress.com/2013/10/22/johnny-tremain-esther-forbes-book-review/.

MOVIEGUIDE, review of *A Cinderella Story*, https://www.movieguide.org/reviews/a-cinderella-story.html.

MOVIEGUIDE, review of *Lord of the Rings: The Return of the King*, https://www.movieguide.org/reviews/the-lord-of-the-rings-the-return-of-the-king.html.

MOVIEGUIDE, review of *The Perfect Man*, https://www.movieguide.org/reviews/the-perfect-man.html.

Harper Collins Alexander, "The Mortal Instruments—The City of Bones—Cassandra Clare—Book Review," August 24, 2013, https://christianbookreviewsblog.wordpress.com/2013/08/24/the-city-of-bones-book-review/.

UNIT 6

Making Connections: "Be a Man"

Helen Rowland, *A Guide to Men: Being Encore Reflections of a Bachelor Girl* (New York: Dodge Publishing, 1922; Project Gutenberg, 2009), https://www.gutenberg.org/files/30630/30630-h/30630-h.htm, 28 [first quotation], 44 [second quotation], 94 [third quotation].

Making Connections: "Be a Woman"

Amy Chozick quoting Hillary Clinton in "Hillary Clinton and the Return of the (Unbaked) Cookies," *New York Times*, November 5, 2016, https://www.nytimes.com/2016/11/06/us/politics/hillary-clinton-cookies.html.

Olivia B. Waxman quoting Toni Morrison in "Toni Morrison Dies: Inspiring Words from the Beloved Author," *Time* online, August 6, 2019, https://time.com/5606750/toni-morrison-inspiring-quotes/.

UNIT 7

Community Organizations

Miracle Hill Ministries Mission Statement, 2019, https://miraclehill.org/who-we-are/.

UNIT 8

Case Study: Social Media and Culture

Mark Zuckerberg, "Building Global Community,"
Facebook published note, February 16, 2017, https://
www.facebook.com/notes/mark-zuckerberg/building
-global-community/10154544292806634/.

PHOTO CREDITS

COVER

Front drbimages/iStock/Getty Images Plus/Getty Images; **Back** Mix and Match Studio/Shutterstock.com

UNIT 1

1 Elena_Mikhailova/iStock/Getty Images Plus/Getty Images; **2** ollirg/iStock/Getty Images/Getty Images Plus; **9** FLHC 56/Alamy Stock Photo/Patrick Mahoney

UNIT 2

15 (Latin Vulgate) Chronicle/Alamy Stock Photo; **15** (Wycliffe) Public Domain; **15** (Gutenberg) "Gutenberg"/Wikimedia Commons/Public Domain; **15** (Gutenberg manuscript) Age Fotostock/Heinz-Dieter Falkenstein/Media Bakery; **15** (Greek manuscript) Werner Forman/Universal Images Group/Getty Images; **15** (Tyndale) Print Collector/Hulton Fine Art Collection/Getty Images; **16**t DEA / G. DAGLI ORTI/De Agostini/Getty Images; **16**ct © Look and Learn / Bridgeman Images; **16**cb Matthew's Bible/British Library; **16**b "King-James-Version-Bible-first-edition-title-page-1611"/Wikimedia Commons/Public Domain

UNIT 3

53t "The Night Watch - HD"/Wikimedia Commons/Public Domain; **53**c "Tsunami by hokusai 19th century"/Wikimedia Commons/Public Domain; **53**b "John Constable - The Hay Wain (1821)"/Wikimedia Commons/Public Domain; **54**t "Wassily Kandinsky Composition VII"/Wikimedia Commons/Public Domain; **54**c Picasso, Pablo (1881-1973) © ARS, NY Daniel-Henry Kahnweiler, autumn 1910. Oil on canvas, 39 9/16 x 28 9/16 in. (100.4 x 72.4 cm). Gift of Mrs. Gilbert W. Chapman in memory of Charles B. Goodspeed, 1948.561. © 2020 Estate of Pablo Picasso / Artists Rights Society (ARS), New York/The Art Institute of Chicago / Art Resource, NY; **54**b Universal History Archive/Universal Images Group/Getty Images

UNIT 4

71t PEDRE/E+/Getty Images; **71**b Anadolu Agency/Anadolu/Getty Images

UNIT 5

95 Twinsterphoto/Shutterstock.com